My friend Chad is giving us ████████ full of grace and truth. Over the p████ ██ has been a divorce between grace and truth amongst many believers. God is shaking the temple and bringing believers together, so the world will experience a God that looks like Jesus. Jesus, who is the Truth, will set you free. How free would you like to be? Read this book slowly, then let it read you.

LEIF HETLAND
President, Global Mission Awareness
Author of *Called to Reign* and *Healing the Orphan Spirit*

As the Charismatic stream of the church moves through its coming-of-age phase, spiritual fathers like Chad Norris are being called forth to speak not what so many in the church want to hear, but what they need to hear. In this, his latest book, *God is Shaking His Temple*, with his characteristic frankness and vulnerability, Chad addresses issues that those with ears to hear would be wise to heed. Chad is a man after God's heart, who desires to steward with wisdom what God is doing on the earth through His Bride. Thank you, Chad for the courage to say what you hear the Father saying.

SUSAN THOMPSON
Author, Editor
Revelation Writing

I met Chad Norris when I read his first book and had him as a guest on my podcast. After that initial conversation, I added him to the shortlist of authors whose messages have profoundly impacted my life. Chad has navigated many peaks and valleys the past few years as God has walked him through an extended season of purging and refining to birth this message in him. My prayer is that this book will spark an insatiable hunger for the deep things of God that come at a great cost, a life marked by reverence, holiness, and a healthy fear of the Lord.

SHAUN TABATT

Publishing Executive, Destiny Image

Chad Norris is God's change agent on the earth. I believe that this book is an apostolic message to the church. The days of sugarcoating the gospel are over!

Get ready for Chad to challenge your doctrine and theology and call you to repentance. It's time to return to the Lord, fully. It's time for the temple to be shaken.

APOSTLE MALIK EDWARDS

Senior leader of Malik Edwards ministries,

Relentless and the Surge Network.

It is rare that I come across a book that reminds me of the God of Heaven that I have earnestly tried to explain in my writings after meeting Jesus following my own clinical death several years ago, but Chad Norris' book, *God is Shaking His Temple,* did just that. Chad not only reminded me of the God I met in Heaven, he also challenged me with the immense calling that God has placed upon each of us. In this way, *God is Shaking His Temple* stands as exceptional amongst the great books of reformation in the Body of Christ's history. My experience is that many describe God in trite terms that tend to trivialize the vastness of God's character, and likewise God's purpose for us oftentimes gets lost in traditions that tend to obfuscate the depth of the church's highest calling. But clearly Chad has cut through any trivial pursuits of God by cutting to the core of who God is and what God has charged us to do in this world. *Finally*, I thought to myself while reading Chad's book, *someone gets Him, and what He wants to do.* I love Chad's spiritually raw honesty and depth of understanding. Surely this book must be read by anyone desiring to honor God with their body, soul, and spirit. Moreover, I believe Chad's revelatory insights are a clarion call to revolutionize the modern era Western church so that God can pour forth His revival throughout this world. When I met Chad not too long ago, I sensed a story in him that was a directive from God's throne—a fresh awakening – and this book is that story. *God is Shaking His Temple* is well-written and entertaining and convicting and liberating. I not only recommend this exceptional book—I would list it to any one serious about their faith as required reading. It is that important. Thank you, Chad, for gifting us with what I consider as a direct message from God—the One I met in Heaven.

RANDY KAY
Author, *Revelations From Heaven*
Founder, Randy Kay Ministries (randykay.org)

In every generation God raises up voices that communicate the raw intention of Heaven and who carry a father's mantle for the next generation beyond them. Without a doubt, I believe Pastor Chad Norris is indeed an apostolic father in hosting the presence and gathering generations into God's storyline of revival. This new book is a must-have in your spiritual arsenal. I have been marked personally by God is *Shaking His Temple* as it not just a literary work but the overflow of the daily lifestyle and conviction of this phenomenal author and leader.

TORREY MARCEL HARPER
Pastor & Itinerant Prophet
Habitation NYC
www.globalprayernyc.org

GOD IS SHAKING HIS TEMPLE

The Fear of the Lord is Returning to the Church

CHAD NORRIS

DESTINY IMAGE® PUBLISHERS, INC.
P.O. Box 310, Shippensburg, PA 17257-0310
"Promoting Inspired Lives."

This book and all other Destiny Image and Destiny Image Fiction books are available at Christian bookstores and distributors worldwide.

Cover design by Blake Berg
Interior design by Terry Clifton

For more information on foreign distributors, call 717-532-3040.
Reach us on the Internet: www.destinyimage.com.

ISBN 13 TP: 978-0-7684-6096-4
ISBN 13 eBook: 978-0-7684-6097-1
ISBN 13 HC: 978-0-7684-6099-5
ISBN 13 LP: 978-0-7684-6098-8

For Worldwide Distribution, Printed in the U.S.A.
1 2 3 4 5 6 7 8 / 26 25 24 23 22 21

DEDICATION

I love you, Wendy, and I'm proud of the wife, mom, and leader you are. Who would have ever thought that what He has had us walk and lead through would end up being better than two trips to Colorado for marriage therapy? Leading here with you through the ups and downs of ministry has brought us closer together, and I'm excited about many more years of leading out together. Your writing career is about to take off and, like I've said many times, and you will go so much further than me with the pen. I'll sincerely be your biggest fan. I love you, Budweina.

Sammy, you are ready for this next stage. You are a grown man in an eighteen-year-old body. I'll cheer you on as you follow Him with whatever He has for you. Being your dad is honestly one of the greatest honors of my life. I'm really proud of you for not being the typical cynical pastor's kid. You are loyal to your Heavenly Father, and you are a great example to your siblings.

Ruthie, I'm so dang proud of you and the young lady you are becoming. You are fierce like your mama, and I still thank the Father for giving me a girl. You light up our house, and you may be my favorite. Don't tell the boys. There is a big call on you, Boofus, and your mom and I will be here to help steward the gift He has given you. You are not allowed to get married until you are fifty. Be at peace.

Jack Jack, hanging out with you is one of my favorite hobbies. You keep me young, and your enthusiasm and spunk give our house a childlike passion. I have a prophetic hunch that you will be a kid when you are a hundred years old. As Sammy is leaving the home, you make it easier because we can hang out. I will never forget what happened to you under the tent when Torrey prayed for you. God is so good. It will be the greatest privilege of my life to watch what God does with you and your siblings.

Father, You scooped me up when I was in shambles, and You put me back together. I want to finish what You have for me down here, but I sincerely can't wait for the day I make a beeline to hug You. You are the Most High God and my Father! I still can't get over that. Thank You, a million times over.

ACKNOWLEDGMENTS

I want to thank Susan Thompson for once again making me a much better writer than I really am. Let's be honest, Susan, these last two books have had some serious help from you. What I appreciate about you is that you love the Father with every cell in your body. Writing is so much more enjoyable for me knowing that you are a part of my book projects. You help me not only write, but also work stuff out in my own heart as I go. I hope we get to work together many more times.

Thank you to Andy and Annwen Stone. Countless conversations with you two have helped me craft so many thoughts about what has been inside of my belly for so long concerning discipleship. I tell Wendy often that you both are the most Christian people I think I know. I've never met two people who have taken Matthew 28:19 more serious than the both of you. You will always been in debt to me for hiring you two to work in a climate with so much sunshine. Don't ever forget that, Andrew. Sisson is somewhere in England right now still mad about the rain.

Thank you to Michael and Amber Thornton—thank you from the bottom of my heart. When you two brought your family of seven here, I knew that God was writing a story that only He can get credit for. The passion you both carry for the tent and the fire are contagious. Michael, I'll never forget that conversation on the mountain where Holmes started that school. God has big plans for you both, and I am overwhelmed with tears when I think about what you two have done for Wendy and me on a personal level. Michael, you brought healing to me at a time when I wondered if I could even go on in ministry. I will never be able to say thank you enough.

Thank you to Dave Rhodes. You introduced me to paradox. When all of this is over, what we have is our memories. I have some great memories with you along the way. What's better than Wayfarer may be those Championships in Thomson. When my two boys get older, we will have to show them how to win the big one. Making another run with you would be fun. Thank you for helping me see both sides of the coin. You even putt left handed, for Heaven's sake.

Thank you to the elders at Bridgeway Church. Without you men, I would not be allowed to be an out-of-the-box leader. You guys have followed me as I've listened to the Father on what it is that He has for us to build out. Y'all have harnessed me, challenged me, and at times kept me from making some poor decisions. I will never be able to say thank you enough. TJ, that morning at Eggs Up will go down as a pivotal time in the history of my leadership. Without you, I would not be the leader I am today. To all of you—we have bonded through trials, and I can honestly say that I thank God often for each of you "lions." Seriously, thank you!

Thank you to Bridgeway Church. Pastoring this church the past seven years has been the hardest and most rewarding experience in my lifetime. Pastoring here has kept me close to the one I want to please. Let's stay focused and finish well. I hope I'm here a long time to be a part of what the Father has started with us.

Ascent University. You students have no idea the joy and purpose y'all bring to me. I can't believe I get to be a part of this. There is nothing I've ever done that has given me more joy than watching each of you ascend His mountain. We are just getting started. I can't wait to see what He has in store for us. Each of you have played a role in stirring my hunger for Him in ways I can't describe. Thank you from the bottom of my heart.

CONTENTS

Foreword 1

Introduction 5

CHAPTER 1   Tension 19

CHAPTER 2   Severity 31

CHAPTER 3   Confrontation 43

CHAPTER 4   Messy Harvest 59

CHAPTER 5   Rebuke 71

CHAPTER 6   Idolatry 87

CHAPTER 7   The Judgment Seat of Christ 101

CHAPTER 8   The Forgotten Commandment 119

CHAPTER 9   Reformation 133

CHAPTER 10   Multiplication 149

CHAPTER 11   Tent: Gathering around His Presence 161

CHAPTER 12   Home: Creating Discipleship Community 173

CHAPTER 13   City: Going into All the World 193

EPILOGUE   Restoring the Fear of the Lord in the Church . . . 207

FOREWORD

love Chad Norris. His heart for the Church is infectious. I have had the privilege of witnessing firsthand Chad's passion as he leads his church with hunger, revelation, integrity, and a desire for the presence of God. Chad's latest book, *God is Shaking His Temple,* while also inspiring and inviting us to step into the current reformation and embrace what God is doing in this new season. My conviction is that this book will mark you, just as knowing Chad has marked me.

Chad begins with his personal story of encountering the love of the Father and the revelation of just how much our heavenly Father loves each one of us. This revelation changed him forever, setting him on a new trajectory as he dug deeper and deeper, learning and growing in his understanding of who God is. His own life experiences, testimonies, dramatic encounters, and words from the Lord are woven throughout the book contextualizing his revelations and making them personal and relatable, and creating a beautiful context for us to experience the Father ourselves.

Chad's compelling journey into the heart of God leads to the holiness of God, reminding us that Jesus is the way to the Father, who is a kind and loving Father, but also one who is Holy and to be revered. This revelation of the holiness of God is often missing from the Body of Christ but is imperative to understanding who God is.

Chad reminds us of the importance of being ready for the second coming of Jesus, a preparedness that comes from truly knowing Him and remaining in His grace as we continue to grow in the fear of the Lord. He fervently calls the

Church to return to its first love and the heart and mission of God even if that means reprioritizing the very ways in which we do church. This book is a trumpet call not to get caught up in the chaos of our nation and the world, but to continue tuning into what God is saying and doing through the sacrifice of corporate worship, passionate prayer gatherings and absolute obedience to Jesus' voice and call, whatever the cost.

Chad does not shy away from the challenges the Church is facing today. In these pages he gives us tools to navigate the climate of our day as followers of Jesus. It is through this equipping that I believe we will see a much-needed return to holiness within the Church and a resolute steadfastness that will have us standing firm in who we are and whose we are. It is impossible to walk away from this book without feeling provoked, shaken, and stirred for the heart of God and His Bride. Get ready, your life will never be the same!

DUNCAN SMITH
President of Catch The Fire World
Author of *Consumed With Holy Fire*

INTRODUCTION

grew up Baptist. If someone had told me what my life would look like down the road, I never would have believed them. I had my own ideas. I told God early on that I would not pastor a church. Well, God did not pay much attention to what I said I would and would not do. After finishing seminary and realizing that I was indeed going to pastor a church, I figured I would be the next-in-line Reformed pastor to honor the tradition of John Calvin and the rest of the Protestant Reformers. Again, God had other plans.

Paul never saw his destiny coming.

It happened in 2002. In one dramatic encounter I became a Charismatic. I had an open vision of Jesus Christ, received the baptism of the Holy Spirit, and immediately began to speak in tongues. Within six months I saw blind eyes open when I prayed for a woman named Gail. When studying the life of Paul, what stands out to me most is how Paul never saw his destiny coming. To say that he was shocked when the Lord blinded him is an understatement. Paul's journey took an abrupt turn. As I look back on the last twenty years of my journey with God, I still shake my head at the abrupt turns along the way.

I grew up not believing in signs, wonders, or miracles. As a matter of fact, I grew up in legalism. Let me just be clear in saying that I have no desire to ever venture back into that world. I actually enjoy when God does strange things to offend the religious mind. He offended my religious mind, and it changed me profoundly in the very best way. I have seen angelic feathers fall on people when I pray for them, gold dust appear, and at times I have literally felt the winds of the angelic blow into a room during a service or times of public ministry. God has placed me in situations where His supernatural manifests to people who are not even open to the supernatural. I have published two books on the kindness of the Father.

To say that He saved my life is an understatement. God the Father healed me of a nervous breakdown, delivered me from heavy medications (Zoloft, Xanax, Klonopin), and now uses me to help a lot of people walk in friendship with Him. I lead a Charismatic church called Bridgeway Church in Greenville, South Carolina, and we have a university called Ascent that has local and online students who are hungry to walk in friendship with God.

I am almost fifty years old, have been married twenty-four years, and have three kids and a dog that needs therapy. There is nothing fancy about me, and I want to tell you up front I am not a deconstructionist. Not only do I not think I have all of the answers, but I believe in the bottom of my heart that I put Jesus Christ on that cross. I am a broken leader who identifies more with Henri Nouwen's works than I do people who have never been through their own dark night of the soul. My wife and I say often that the people who speak into our marriage and our own lives are those who have been through their own crucibles and have come out on the other side bruised, healed, and closer to the Father.

I am going to say some very strong things in this book that have been written through tears and hundreds of conversations with real people with real problems who just want to know God. As Nouwen said, "I am simply a wounded healer." Sometimes healing looks a little different than we want it to. There are times that the Father brings a word of correction that does not feel good. I believe the Charismatic church is in a season of correction right now that does not feel good.

What I have noticed over the last eight years of pastoring Bridgeway Church is that there has been a message that infiltrated the Charismatic stream of the church that, in my opinion, is the most dangerous teaching the church has ever seen. That may seem like an overstatement to you, but if you will allow me to explain myself perhaps you will be inspired to at least search the Scriptures on the message I am about to bring here.

> **The Father disciplines those He loves, and that is what the Father is currently doing.**

I graduated in 1999 from Beeson Divinity School with an M.Div., and I am close to finishing my doctoral degree at Regent University. I am not just writing this book from experience or even prophetic unction. I have spent the last decade studying the subject I am addressing, and I believe now is the time to write on the judgment at hand from the Father for the Spirit-filled stream of the church. The Father disciplines those He loves, and that is what the Father is currently doing in this amazing stream I so dearly love.

The number 111 have been showing up in my life on a consistent basis for the last five years. When I say consistent, I mean it has gotten to the point where it is borderline eerie. Everywhere I go I see the numbers 111. One day I stopped and said, "Father, what in the world is this all about?" He said:

> Chad, My assignment on you at this juncture is to rebuke, correct, and train. It's what true fathers do. Many men have called themselves fathers or have even been called fathers by others, but they are unwilling to enter conflict and show My church the error of its ways. True fathers make disciples and are not afraid to train through compassion and conflict. I am leading you to the teeth of the dog. I will use you and others to help clean up Charismatic rubbish, to correct erroneous teaching that has infiltrated the church. Many will dislike you for it.

> The fear of the Lord is returning center stage. You and Wendy listened to Carol Arnott speak years ago at Bethel Church about the fear of the Lord returning to the church, and that time is now. I am dismantling My church and I am bringing correction. I am shaking My church. That time is now.

The Father then led me to Revelation 1:11. Needing some clarity on this number business, I called a seasoned prophet, someone God has used all over the world. I told him what was going on and then asked him what he thought God was saying to me. He proceeded to prophesy that there was a Jacob's ladder anointing on my life, and that the angelic would begin to ascend and descend in my ministry in more noticeable ways. From the day that he prophesied that over me until now, there has been a strong shift in my encounters in the Word, a strong shift in my encounters with the Lord in my dreams, and a strong shift in my times of public prophecy. There has also been a sharpness in my encounters with God. Thankfully I have had the Father's words in Isaiah 6:1-8 to bless and guide me like a rudder in the midst of all of this shifting, shaking, and sharpness. But let me backtrack a little.

My yearning for Jesus took me to a place in 1996 where I did not have to exegete the Scriptures to understand Isaiah 6. Isaiah 6 interpreted me. It was on the campus of a university in Campbellsville, Kentucky. One day the pure power and glory of God came into my room. To say that I thought I might die is not an exaggeration. His magnificent and indescribable glory literally threw me to the floor. I have never felt more inadequate than I did at that moment. I thought His presence was going to kill me. I wept violently, and I felt the gravity of sin, even though I was not walking in any unconfessed sin or addiction. I simply had an encounter with holiness that I can't describe in words. This experience lasted about an hour when I felt something like a hand touch my head, even though no one else was in the room. I started to laugh uncontrollably with a joy that is hard to describe. At one point I was laughing so hard that I thought I was going to pass out. It would be another nine years before I even heard of what God did in Toronto with holy laughter. A friend of mine came looking for me, and when he walked into my room, he fell on his face and began to cry hard. The pure holiness in that room was honestly terrifying.

Since that day I have not once asked God to do anything like that to me again. I sometimes wonder why so many Charismatics focus so much on what the devil is up to. Just one profound revelation of the fear of the Lord would have them giving zero time to the devil and his tactics and all their time and attention to God.

> **With spiritual reformation comes spiritual warfare.**

Fast-forward to now. As I look at my current assignment to rebuke, correct, and train, it makes sense that my first encounter with the Most High God was an Isaiah 6 moment. Verse 4 says, *"And the foundations of the thresholds shook at the voice of him who called, and the house was filled with smoke"* (ESV). Anyone who has eyes to see will find the God of Isaiah 6 once again shaking His church to its foundations in this season. There is a move of God at hand, and it is not revival. This move is not an outpouring from Heaven, nor is it a visitation. This move of God is a reformation. In times of reformation there is tremendous turbulence, disagreement, and collision. Many people will think that in the coming days the devil will be very active in God's church. If you will look closer and draw your ear to the Word and to the voice of the Father, He will show you that He is the one behind this shaking.

With spiritual reformation comes spiritual warfare. This is a time in history when the words of Jesus Christ in Matthew chapter 10 ring ever so loudly.

> *"Do not suppose that I have come to bring peace to the earth. I did not come to bring peace, but a sword. For I have come to turn 'a man against his father, a daughter against her mother, a daughter-in-law against her mother-in-law—a man's enemies will be the members of his own household'"* (Matthew 10:34-36).

What once was a staple in the church of Jesus Christ (fear of the Lord) is now seen as spiritual abuse by so many in the Charismatic stream. With so much emphasis on the message of sonship in the Body of Christ, we are now seeing the pendulum swing far in the extreme, with rebellion running rampant in the Lord's church. Freedom has become confused with lawlessness. Conversations on spiritual authority and submission are quickly labeled as control and abuse. We have lost Jesus in a stream that bears His name.

Where have all of the Watchman Nees gone? Where are the Dietrich Bonhoeffers? Where are the Pauls? We have many well-known ministers with platforms and influence, but where are the fathers who disciple? I mean truly disciple the next generation into friendship with God. You can't make a disciple from a stage, a podcast, a movie, or a book. True biblical discipleship is life, on life and it is messy. Where are the disciple-makers who have undeniable fruit of multiplying themselves into other disciples? There are some out there, but far too few. Paul said, *"Even if you had ten thousand guardians in Christ, you do not have many fathers, for in Christ Jesus I became your father through the Gospel"* (1 Cor. 4:15).

A passion for, and submission to, the local church is now seen as an old way of doing things. Podcasts, conferences, and cherry-picking authors replace discipleship by fathers and mothers in the faith who are rooted in the local church and serve by giving their lives away. God is shaking and waking His Bride up, and such a holy shaking will bring division. If you study church history closely, Azusa Street did not bring unity to the church. As a matter of fact, what God did at Azusa changed the world and divided the church greatly. In 1906, God exploded onto the scene in Los Angeles, the City of Angels. Yet if you were living during the time of the outpouring at Azusa in the early 1900s, it would have felt more like a civil war within the church at large than many people make it out to be today as they tell the stories of William Seymour and his team.

There is a judgment at hand in God's church and the one who is leading the charge is Jesus Christ Himself. This reformation move of God will have tremendous fruit globally, but before that happens there is going to be a serious cleansing in the church, and it is coming to the Charismatic stream. Not only will this cleansing not feel good, but it will divide brother against brother and sister against sister. It's actually already started, and when New Testament judgment falls, it is not something to treat lightly. It's hard enough to get a Charismatic to believe that there is such thing as New Testament judgment, yet Simon Peter sure understood it when he said, *"For it is time for judgment to begin with God's household; and if it begins with us, what will the outcome be for those who do not obey the Gospel of God?"* (1 Pet. 4:17).

As the Father began to talk to me over the last ten years about this message, I thought, "This is not going to be received well," and that has certainly been my experience. I would never have thought that so much warfare would be attracted to the message of the fear of the Lord had I not experienced it myself. I have been preaching the fear of the Lord for the last seven years at Bridgeway Church, and I have found it to be the single most divisive subject in my twenty-two years of leadership in ministry. It has been way more divisive than tongues, women in ministry, or the gifts themselves.

> **"Is God always in a good mood?"**
> **No. Is God always good? Yes.**

Revelation 1:11 served as the gateway to this assignment on me. It says: *"Write on a scroll what you see and send it to the seven churches: to Ephesus, Smyrna, Pergamum, Thyatira, Sardis, Philadelphia and Laodicea."* Well, to five of these seven churches in the New Covenant age, Jesus was not happy with them, which leads me to ask, "Is God always in a good mood?" No. Is God always good? Yes. Sometimes, however, His goodness comes through His severity. Are we as clean as Jesus in our righteousness because of Calvary if we are His disciples? Yes. Does that mean that the Holy Spirit only convicts us of our righteousness? No.

Where has our reverence for God gone? How did the church drift away from understanding that we are small before Father God? Yes, His goodness and mercy endure forever, but in order to fully appropriate these aspects of His character, we need to abandon ourselves to Him, trusting Him from a posture of humility and respect.

Every Christmas holiday my family watches the movie *Elf.* A few years ago, as I was laughing out loud at something Will Ferrell did in the movie, the Father spoke to me and said, "Many of My children see Me more like Buddy the Elf than who I really am." I don't know about you, but I don't see God in tights. Proverbs 9:10 says, *"The fear of the Lord is the beginning of wisdom, and the knowledge of the Holy One is insight"* (ESV). God is *holy.* We need to stand in awe of Him. God intends that we live full, fruitful lives. In Jesus we have a hope and a future, and we can most clearly see that hope and that future from a posture of true humility.

It is time for the church to wake up, especially the Charismatic stream of the church. The Charismatic stream of the church has been stuck in a coming-of-age stage for so long that the Father is now putting the foot of reformation on our backs as He pushes us into maturity. Whether or not we know this, there is a judgment at hand now, and that judgment is coming from the Lord Himself. What excites me the most about all of this is that when God disciplines His own, it is actually for our good. Is it possible that on the other side of this reformation judgment, there is a real and powerful move of God that so many of us have been crying out for? What if this cleansing, this maturation, is the preparation needed for the genuine end-time harvest that so many have prophesied?

Many leaders in the Lord's church are sensing a massive move of God coming. I am one of those leaders. Yet before a great move of God comes to the earth, I believe He is going to cleanse His church, because we need cleansing. There are many contaminants in the Charismatic stream that God Himself is cleaning out. I prophesied from the stage three years ago that God was going to begin to remove pastors from their positions and tear down the stages of itinerant leaders who have given the celebrity spirit a stronghold in the church. There is judgment from Heaven at hand, and that judgment is starting in God's church. Come, Lord Jesus!

Chapter 1

TENSION

My nervous breakdown seems like a lifetime ago to me. Years of clinical depression and anxiety culminated into one horrific season when I simply could not cope with life anymore. I remember being curled up on the kitchen floor, wondering if life would ever go back to normal again. I had tapered off of some high-powered medications for depression and anxiety too quickly, and my body did not respond well. What ensued was a nightmare.

My brain had a buzzing feeling, and I had a hard time completing a sentence without having to really think through what I was saying. I had night sweats, tremors in my hands, and was experiencing feelings of utter terror in my mind and heart. Unless you've been there, it's really difficult to explain. I had an almost impossible time sleeping, and when I was awake, I felt like a zombie. It was in this season that Jesus healed me and showed me the kindest person I have ever met in my life. Up until then, when I thought about God I thought of a busy, distant figure who had more important things to do than connect with me in any meaningful way. I believed that He was real and that He helped with big decisions in life, but when it came to anything personal, the Father of Jesus Christ was not someone I knew. I was more comfortable with Jesus than I was with His Father. In many ways, God the Father was someone I was actually terrified of. I had an utter terror impression of God instead of a holy fear of the Father, and as a result I did not want much to do with Him. I interacted with Him as little as possible, just enough to get that "insurance" needed so as not to spend an eternity in hell. As far as relationship went, being intimate with Him was not something that was a part of my experience. That all changed quickly, and I never saw it coming.

If You've Seen Me, You've Seen the Father

One day in a counseling session with a trained therapist, something happened to me that changed my life forever. My wife and I were sitting in a room in Titusville, Florida, talking to this therapist when all of a sudden I went into a vision and saw Jesus Christ. Since then I have had many impressions from God, and He has taught me how to walk in the prophetic. Yet what happened in that moment in Florida was not an impression. It was a literal open vision, much like watching a movie in real time. I felt like I was being transported somewhere.

> **The love radiating from Him knocked me out of my chair and poured through my body wave upon wave.**

Jesus stood there in front of me and said, "Chad, I am your Healer, trust Me." He said that twice to me. The love radiating from Him knocked me out of my chair and poured through my body wave upon wave. There were two angels standing with Him, one taller than the other. The tall one had a sword. I will never forget my first thought when I came to my senses and the vision ended: *If you have seen Me, you have seen the Father.* I had just encountered the Father in the person of Jesus Christ. I knew from Hebrews 1 that Jesus is the exact representation of the Father. Yet in all my years I was so deceived that I did not believe it. In that moment I knew that I had some serious soul and Scripture searching to do.

My wife was with me in that counseling session when this encounter happened. When I came to, I looked at her and did not know what to say. Despite the fact that I had been to many sessions of counseling trying to deal with the fact that I believed I was rotten at my core and that God was not pleased with me, I still struggled to relate to God. Around six months before this experience with Jesus, I was led to read Jerry Bridges' book *Transforming Grace*. Because of what I had read, I slowly—and I mean slowly—started to believe that God didn't hate me. Now, after this encounter with Jesus, I immediately knew that I had been deceived all of my life about who God is and who I am in relation to Him through Jesus. I am still moved to tears all these years later simply thinking about the fact that the God of the universe loves me.

After this encounter, I became very hungry to search the Scriptures. The more I dug into Paul's letters and the Gospel of John, specifically, the more the lights started coming on for me. The Father loved me! I felt like I was in some sort of new life. I had given my life to Jesus Christ at the age of twelve, but after this experience I was getting born again, again. I realize that this is not theologically correct, but that is what it felt like to me.

I began to read every single passage in the ministry of Jesus differently. Every time I saw Him going about and forgiving people or healing people, I began to think of His actions as coming from the Father Himself. Something began to happen to me, and it did not take long for me to see the fruit of this inner change in my heart. I simply could not believe what the Holy Spirit was showing me as it related to the nature of God. I started to fall in love with God the Father. I would cry when reflecting upon passages like Colossians 1:21-22, which says that Jesus actually presented me before the Father and I am now accepted and cherished. I would put my name in these passages and personalize them. "Chad was once alienated and hostile in mind, but now Jesus has presented Chad before the Father and presented him as holy." Some days I felt like I was going to burst with joy.

When you go your entire life believing deep down that Calvary was only about appeasing the wrath of a holy God and that He does not like you, it can lead you down some dark paths. Even with a master of divinity degree, I carried zero revelation of the kindness of the Father. I blame no one for this, but the reality was that I was a lost spiritual orphan with the position of righteousness and zero experience of the benefits of my right standing with God.

> **Even with a master of divinity degree, I carried zero revelation of the kindness of the Father.**

I will never forget when an evangelist came through our church talking about hell and the reality of living an eternity away from God. I took what he was saying to such a place that I created an image of God in my heart that was inaccurate. I formed an image of a God who would forgive me and allow me to come to Heaven when I died, but in the meantime God was always upset with me. I would shake when I went past a cemetery. I dreaded the thought of letting God down on an everyday basis. Thankfully, my encounter with Jesus changed everything for me.

After my encounter with Jesus the Son, He led me to the Father through the Word itself. I read the Gospel of John more than a thousand times, and as I did my experience with the Father changed. Within one year, I saw blind eyes open when I prayed for a lady named Gail. The kindness of the Father led me from a fetal position on the floor in my kitchen in front of my wife to praying for a blind woman and seeing her healed. I have ministered on the message of Abba Father hundreds of times since then and have had so many miraculous experiences that many of you would probably have a hard time believing me. I believe that Romans 2:4 describes it well when it says: *"Or do you show contempt for the riches of his kindness, forbearance and patience, not realizing that God's kindness is intended to lead you to repentance?"*

We need to understand that His kindness is supernatural. I have seen this to be true again and again. I believe in John 14:12. I have been to Haiti several times to minister and have seen the miraculous loving-kindness of God touch and heal. God has taken me around the world and to many different places in America where I have not only preached the Word, but I have also seen the supernatural of God manifest when

I pray for people. For me, the book of Acts is not just an historical account of supernatural things that the disciples did many years ago. It is real for us today.

I don't ask for supernatural things to happen when I pray. What God does in response to my prayers is up to Him. I was praying over a pastor once, and as I was prophesying about his role in the city, five blue feathers fell on him. We were indoors and no birds had flown over us. This pastor is not Charismatic; he wasn't looking for signs. Mark 16:17 says that signs will follow those who believe. I have had quite a number of experiences of feathers falling as I pray for people. I don't know why feathers. It seems to be one way God shows His presence in those moments.

> Since the Holy Spirit started showing me who the Father really is, I have yet to get over it.

The Father is the kindest person I've ever known. I am constantly overcome by His tenderness. Sometimes when His love manifests in a room it becomes hard for me to minister. How I would love to go back and live my life from the beginning with this revelation of the Father's love. Since the Holy Spirit started showing me who the Father really is, I have yet to get over it. His kindness is simply overwhelming. What I am writing about now comes from twenty years of experience walking with the Father as the closest friend I have ever had. I think about Him every day and sometimes yearn to be with Him forever, in a homesick sort of way.

After my encounter with Jesus, I was immediately led into a ten-year journey into sonship, identity, and power. I traveled to many places, preaching the message of the kindness of the Father, and saw hundreds of literal healings as I prayed for people. I took First Corinthians 14:1 very seriously, with a yearning to grow in the prophetic. As it turns out, the prophetic is the strongest gift I operate in. There is nothing I enjoy more than training people to hear the Father's voice because His voice is life-giving and life-changing. Yet, despite the strength of the gift of prophecy on my life, moving and teaching in the prophetic is not my current assignment. God has assigned me to be a leader who stands in the middle of both His kindness and His severity. Paul puts it this way in Romans 11:22: *"Notice how God is both kind and severe. He is severe toward those who disobeyed, but kind to you if you continue to trust in his kindness. But if you stop trusting, you also will be cut off"* (NLT).

I am constantly growing in my ability to hold in tension both a passion for the message of the Father's kindness and His severity. If you want a recipe for going into a deep place in God, read Brennan Manning's book *Abba's Child* and Watchman Nee's book *Spiritual Authority* at the same time. It will make your head spin in a good way. When we are in tension, we grow. Graham Cooke is someone who has been a literary mentor to me and is still greatly influencing me as a leader. Graham says that God has the sunniest disposition of anyone he's ever met. I love that, and it is true that God is so kind. Yet in the book of Acts, God killed two people for lying to Him. God also killed Herod—he was eaten with worms.

Both of these stories are in the New Covenant. Jesus is not happy with the church in his letters found in Revelation. One of the most difficult things you will ever do is to accept that holding truths of God in tension is the recipe that helps us all grow in Him.

> **When we are in tension, we grow.**

Humans tend to enjoy the thinking patterns of "either or" instead of "both and." In the Charismatic stream, I have pastored people who mostly believe in the "kingdom now" message. I know for me, I absolutely love that message, and I have seen hundreds of times when I have used my own faith in God's grace to see breakthrough manifest in the *now* as a result of thinking and praying that way. Yet why is there not more conversation of the kingdom "still coming"? For example, Paul says that we should work out our own salvation in fear and trembling. Paul uses many words to talk about the idea of finishing well and working so as to not lose the prize that's promised.

Perhaps you have gotten your theology from a teacher who is an "either/or" person. For many of us, we have become so parasitic on other teachers that we interpret the Scriptures through others instead of through the Holy Spirit. Many teachers who only focus on one side of the conversation have led many astray because they teach a partial truth. Is it possible that too much "either or" thinking has gotten the church stuck in a ditch? Is God kind? God is the kindest God I've ever met in my life. He is also severe, and His severity is found in both the Old Testament and the New Testament.

I used to think that Jesus existed to get us out of tension. Now I believe the exact opposite. I have never known anyone who has a higher value for tension than Jesus. It has taken me most of my life to understand how much He valued and still values tension. Without tension, people simply don't grow. Twenty years after my encounter with Him, I have noticed that the last twenty years have been one big journey into paradox. It has been in paradox that I have found the deepest connection with God that I have ever known.

> **I have never known anyone who has a higher value for tension than Jesus.**

I spent four years in Birmingham, Alabama pastoring students in a church that was highly interested in the teachings of John Piper. Until this day some twenty years later, I have not seen another author or teacher influence college-aged disciples like Piper did. His teachings had a tremendous impact on my life as well. I appreciate how much he helped me develop a God-centered perspective. Yet with those same students, if I brought up the name Gregory Boyd, they would look at me like I had nine eyeballs on my forehead. Piper is a five-point Calvinist and Boyd has written on open theism. They are at two ends of the spectrum theologically. During my time pastoring in Alabama, Piper was very vocal about his displeasure with Gregory Boyd, and it caused quite the stir in the church back in the '90s. I had some seriously intense conversations with people over the differences between these two. What I noticed was that very few students were willing to read both of these men.

> I honestly don't know why so many people are afraid of paradox. Do we think that God can be figured out like some sort of formula?

As I look back, I honestly don't know why so many people are afraid of paradox. Do we think that God can be figured out like some sort of formula? I read John Calvin's *Institutes of the Christian Religion* and I greatly respect that contribution to the Kingdom of God. But I simply refuse to honor the Reformed tradition while ignoring what Jacob Arminius brought to the table as well. When is the last time you met someone who read both Charles Spurgeon and John Wesley at the same time? People are typically afraid of paradox. If we are not careful, we will find ourselves entrenched in an extreme truth about God while failing to realize that there is an opposite and equal truth that seems to contradict. Is God kind? Yes. And He is also severe. Many New Covenant Charismatics have built an empire of thought from only the revelation of His kindness. I believe this has created a dangerous trajectory in the church that is causing us to drift further and further away from what is perhaps the greatest revelation any of us can ever have, which is fear of the Lord.

Chapter 2

SEVERITY

will never forget the first time I got a word of knowledge for someone. It was in 2003. When God began to show me that we can talk to Him and He will talk back to us and give us words for other people, it shocked me. At that time in my life, I was not even sure that God liked me very much. I theologically understood the atonement, but I honestly thought it was more about appeasing the Father's wrath than the way for me to step back into an intimate connection with the God of Genesis 1 and 2. I for sure did not think that the Father liked me. As a matter of fact, I did not even call Him Father. To me He was a distant figure who held the keys to Heaven, not my literal Heavenly Father whom I could talk to and walk through this life with.

After my encounter with Jesus that day in counseling, I began to renew my mind through the Gospels and Paul's letters regarding who God is. That's when God began to activate the prophetic in me. I would hear God clearly as He talked to me about others, then I would prophetically share what I was hearing from God as I prayed for people. At times God would show me things about others with such clarity that it shocked me. I was not used to this type of lifestyle in God. The prophetic can be quite shocking, especially if you are not used to it.

At the time, I was sitting under teaching that said God would only call out the gold in people and would never correct someone, especially in front of another person. I was trained in the prophetic to "come in the opposite spirit" of what someone was struggling with. It all seemed to make sense because God is full of love. I figured that Jesus' death on the cross was proof of the ultimate form of love—agape love. The mindset I was under at the time said that God only focuses on who a person is; that God will not call out something that is either "off" or actual sin because all of that is covered by the blood of Jesus. As someone who hated conflict and would do anything to avoid it, this all sounded great to me. It was like the Disney World of the prophetic. Let's just all learn how happy God is with us, how clean we are in His eyes. Let's just focus on our righteousness. Because after all, God only focuses on who Jesus is in us. He will never rebuke or correct us because that would fall under the dreaded idea of condemnation. I had grown up under legalism and thought that God did not like me. When I had an encounter with His love, I swung the pendulum so far in the other direction that I unintentionally stepped into what I now call Disney grace. How wrong I was during that season of my life!

> **When I had an encounter with His love, I swung the pendulum so far in the other direction that I unintentionally stepped into what I now call Disney grace.**

Disney Grace

I love Disney World. Mickey Mouse and I share a birthday. We both made our grand entrance on November 18. Even though Mickey came onto the scene years before I was born, because we share the same birthday, when I was young I confidently declared that I was special because I was born the same day as Mickey. That's a big deal to a five-year-old. All these years later, I still appreciate my special Mickey birthday connection.

The first time we took our family of five to Disney World in Orlando, we had a wonderful time of being together, eating, laughing, and riding all the rides. Some dads I know can't stand the thought of standing in the lines at Disney, but I love it. Disney is near perfect. There is no trash, the lines move efficiently, there's plenty to eat, and you won't find happier employees anywhere. Even the weather in Orlando is sunny, making it a perfect place to vacation. Recently I met a gal in London who had been saving up to take her family to Disney World, because when you live in England the kind of weather you find in Orlando, Florida is enough to cry tears of joy.

I will never forget the time when my daughter was four years old and I held her while she watched the fireworks display. My wife looked over at me and saw me crying. I was "that dad" and was just soaking up moments that I knew I would remember when I was older. Disney is designed to give families seemingly perfect moments, and they rarely disappoint. I took our family to another theme park once. It was not a great experience. It smelled like the backside of an ice cream machine that had been sitting out in the sun. We longed for Disney the whole time we were there.

The entire Disney experience is designed to give families a break from reality. It's complete fantasy. The employees are paid to be the happiest people on earth. But do their personal lives reflect the same values? I seriously doubt it. Chick-fil-A is a Disney-like experience. There are times after I order my food at Chick-fil-A that I feel like I can cure cancer. The employees are trained to be so friendly that it's awkward. I know because I once was an employee there myself. One of the things I love to do at a drive through at Chick-fil-A is to say "my pleasure" before they can say it to me. I love my time at Chick-fil-A so much that it takes discipline not to go there too many times in a week.

Truth is, Disney is a fun experience but it's not a glimpse of real life. Real life looks more like the "other theme park." When you walk into Disney, it's like they blow cinnamon into the air. This is what much of the Charismatic stream of the church is doing. We are presenting a partial truth to millions of people, and over the past 30 years or so we have seen this create an image of God that is not real. Let me just put it this way—a partial image of God is demonic in origin. I believe with all of my heart that satan realized that he could not defeat the church so he just joined it. Parents should not only be concerned with protecting their kids from demonic images in movies and books. We should also be concerned about these "Disney grace" teachings that are leading millions of Charismatics astray.

I am not just a guy who travels from town to town in and out of places. I pastor real people through real life troubles.

I have seen firsthand the destruction of this Disney grace. It ruins lives. I sat down with a young married man in his thirties who started reading an author who focuses on the goodness of God without any room for the severity of God. He was close to losing everything as a result of this theology. Interestingly, I had prophesied a day before this meeting that the Charismatic church is an inch from stepping into Universalism. As we talked, this young man said to me, "I was heading straight toward Universalism." What saved him was revelation of the fear of the Lord.

> **Satan realized that he could not defeat the church so he just joined it.**

God created us in His image, and many leaders in the Charismatic stream are returning that favor. James says that we should be very careful before we say yes to being a teacher because the judgment will be much more severe for teachers of the Word (see James 3:1). Many Charismatics are now in a place after so many years of hearing teachings on sonship that they have landed in the confidence that because God is so good, there is not really any consequence to our sin. I can't tell you how many times I have been told as a pastor, "Chad, you just need a love encounter with the Father." I use my imagination sometimes to picture what it would be like for the apostle Paul to lead a church in the Charismatic stream today. I can't imagine some of the things he would say to redirect the illegal thought patterns that much of the church has found itself in.

The true prophetic is listening to God and saying what He says when He says to say it. Samuel sure did not call out the gold in King Saul. The Lord Jesus Christ did not call the gold out of the church in His letters in the book of Revelation. Paul would be called a spiritual abuser in the church today for kicking people out of faith communities. Jesus Christ Himself would be told today that all He needs is a "love encounter" with the Father for calling fellow religious leaders a "brood of vipers." I can't imagine what fellow believers would do to Paul today for telling John Mark that their journey together was over. I laugh a little at the thought of what some Christians on Facebook would do to Paul over that one.

> **The true prophetic is listening to God and saying what He says when He says to say it.**

Is God kind? He is the kindest person I've ever met. Yet there has been so much of an overemphasis on His kindness that we forget that He is also severe. He's a Father, and good fathers don't just call the gold out in people. Good fathers train, rebuke, encourage, hug, fuss, smile, cry, and at times even get loud with those they are called to lead.

The Father is realigning the Charismatic stream of the church to show that He is not only kind, but He is also severe. The Lord Jesus Christ forgave a woman caught in the act of adultery in John 6. He also told people to be careful not to make a little one stumble. In fact, He said that it would be better to have a millstone thrown around your neck than make a little one stumble. What He's getting at is that you better not cause a little one to stumble and remove themselves from God's plans, alignment, and authority structure. The Father is a father who not only values freedom, but also structure. To understand the Bible, one must understand paradox. In paradox we find tension that keeps us grounded and challenged at the same time. There has been so much of an overemphasis on the heart of the Father that the Charismatic stream has drifted away from the reality of the judgment of His scepter.

I tell people that if they want to experience the personality of God in their everyday lives, they should start with John's Gospel. It is my favorite book. John is known as the beloved of Christ. One of my favorite stories from John's Gospel is when Jesus and the disciples were in the upper room and John put his head on the chest of Jesus. If that is not a picture of intimacy, I don't know what is. I have spent two decades teaching on this Gospel and I have seen thousands of lives impacted as I teach and minister on the Father through the lens of the book of John.

When people think about John, they typically think about someone who was tender and close to Jesus Himself. Yet not many people realize or focus on the fact that this same beloved disciple wrote, *"Whoever believes in the Son has eternal life, but whoever rejects the Son will not see life, for God's wrath remains on them"* (John 3:36). Before you assume that this verse is referring to Heaven, you may want to look again. I have said for years that satan's favorite verse in the New Testament is John 3:16. I believe it is the most misinterpreted verse in the Bible since Guttenberg created the printing press and the Scriptures became available for us all to read. Most people immediately believe that eternal life means going to "a place" when we die. That is not what Jesus was talking about with Nicodemus in the middle of the night in John 3. Eternal life is a picture of close and intimate relationship with God that begins on this side of death, not when we "go up there."

Jesus tells us that we are His friends if we do what He commands us to do. There is a blessing that rests upon a person who not only gives their adoration to God through praise but also through obedience. There are millions of Charismatics who believe that what we do is not as important as what we believe when it comes to pleasing God. Rejecting the Son is not just a rejection of Him and the fact that He died on the cross. Rejecting Jesus is also in play for those who proclaim to be His disciples yet don't do what He tells them to do.

In John 6, we see Jesus preach a very tough thing when He tells Jews that they must drink His blood and eat His flesh. It says in the Scripture that "many disciples deserted Him" (see John 6:60-70). For many of us in the Spirit-filled stream, we put so much emphasis on the goodness of God while ignoring how we place ourselves in a position to actually experience the opposition of our good God when we walk in disobedience. There has been so much teaching on positional righteousness that we have failed to realize that we can be as clean as Jesus positionally but abide more in the devil than in Jesus. Many times we find ourselves with God's hand against us and we think it's the devil.

> **There is a blessing that rests upon a person who not only gives their adoration to God through praise but also through obedience.**

A great deal of deception has entered the church regarding this, so much so that much of what we have come to think is spiritual warfare is actually our own disobedience. I can't tell you how many times I've had to help someone understand that they are not experiencing attacks from the enemy but rather opposition from the Father. We need a fresh look at what repentance is and how it applies to the life of a Spirit-filled believer. If Judas could be that close to Jesus and be that deceived, then we need to sober up and start asking some hard questions.

Good News on Severity

First Peter says:

> *For it is time for judgment to begin with God's household; and if it begins with us, what will the outcome be for those who do not obey the Gospel*

of God? And, "If it is hard for the righteous to be saved, what will become of the ungodly and the sinner?" (1 Peter 4:17-18)

This passage shows me two things. First, judgment is real for those who are in Christ. Second, this type of judgment is actually a good thing because it points to a cleansing. It is very difficult for many of us to wrap our minds around the fact that a loving God can also judge us. Yet with just one small glance at the Scriptures themselves, we see that the New Testament paints the picture of just how real this concept is. This judgment can look like God demoting His own leaders out of their positions of influence. We tend to hear lots of messages on how God promotes people, but the idea of demotion is just as real. When God comes to judge His own house, many times that judgment looks like Him removing leaders from their posts.

Society has drifted to a place where people are so easily offended these days. It is happening in the church too. Many well-meaning Christians are totally closed off to any idea whatsoever of judgment. For example, if you say anything negative about homosexuality being a sin you had better watch out, because not just unbelievers but people who consider themselves disciples of Jesus will quickly call you out as a bigot and someone who has not learned how to love others. As a pastor, I hear people say to me, "Only God can judge my heart." That is one of the quickest ways to identify someone who does not believe in spiritual authority.

Many in the church today refuse to let anyone speak direction or correction into them unless they agree with it or it is perceived as "kind." Sometimes, the kindest thing I can do as a pastor is to help a person see where their life will end up if they keep making the mistakes they are making. The work of spiritual fathers and mothers is hard, just like parenting our children is hard. Many people simply don't believe in any form of judgment from God, so why should they believe it when they hear it from leaders in the church?

> **It is God's judgments that cleanse us so that we can progress from glory to glory.**

It is God's judgments that cleanse us so that we can progress from glory to glory. What we too often fail to realize is that in order for God to take a person into a higher realm of connection with Him, He demands a higher level of consecration. A holy God is not fond of communing and truly implementing a culture of habitation with us when we are not properly consecrated. When the King of Glory comes, there is typically a predictable pattern of preparation before we see the manifestation of His presence. John the Baptist had one assignment—to prepare the way for Jesus—and that is what he did. Before God came to Azusa, He first led many people to pray and prepare the table for the feast that nations would eat off of there. Frank Bartleman prayed Azusa into existence with the help of William Seymour and the team.

Right now, the Father is addressing and removing contaminants in the Charismatic stream of the church. He is not some narcissistic ruler who hates people. This judgment at hand is a cleansing. There is a move coming that God's temple (the church) is not currently in a position to help steward. If you study First Peter 4:17-18, you will find that God's judgment is actually a wonderful thing because the cleansing precedes the arrival of a new manifestation of His presence on the earth. If I knew that royalty was coming to my house for dinner, I can promise you that my wife and I would spend a day preparing our house accordingly. How much more should we be open to the purpose of God's judgments? It is time to take a look at what this means for our lives.

Chapter 3

CONFRONTATION

I don't remember a time in my life when I did not have a burning desire to know God. When I say "know Him," I am referring to a literal, deep connection with God that would be considered deep friendship with Him. I lost my hero when I was just five years old. My grandfather—I called him Papa— died of a heart attack. The week he died, I lay in a field on my back and looked up at the sky and thought, "I want to know the God he went to." This was seven years before I would make a public declaration of my faith in Jesus Christ, but on that day in 1977, I lay in that field and deeply pondered who God was and what He was like.

Like most everyone, my life has taken many twists and turns since that day, yet here I am still burning with that same desire to know God better. I never wanted to pastor a church or even author a book. I would have bet a lot of money that I would have gone into coaching an athletic team because I grew up the son of a football coach. Sports have always been a part of my life. Yet, as God would have it, I am now into my twenty-fifth year of leadership in ministry, and I'm thankful that I still want to be close friends with the God I will see with my own eyes one day.

Both the prophet Jeremiah and the apostle Paul had the same desire to know God that has burned in me since I was a little boy. Jeremiah said it this way:

> *This is what the Lord says: "Don't let the wise boast in their wisdom, or the powerful boast in their power, or the rich boast in their riches. But*

> *those who wish to boast should boast in this alone: that they truly* **know me** *and understand that I am the Lord who demonstrates unfailing love and who brings justice and righteousness to the earth, and that I delight in these things. I, the Lord, have spoken!* (Jeremiah 9:23-24 NLT)

The Hebrew word for *know* in this passage is *yada,* and this word points to a deep and intimate connection between one person and another. God desires to be intimately connected to His people. This desire is truly remarkable when one realizes how passionate and full of love God is for us. The apostle Paul said the same thing in a different way when he said, "*I want to know Christ—yes, to know the power of his resurrection and participation in his sufferings, becoming like him in his death*" (Phil. 3:10).

The Greek word for *know* here is the word *ginosko*, which was a Jewish idiom for sexual intimacy inside of the context of marriage. Paul was obviously not talking about this, but the intent behind him saying it this way was to show that he desired the highest level of connection with God possible. We are wired by God for connection with Him, which is why there is a longing inside every human that is not satisfied until we find that connection. We tend to drift from one disappointment to the next until we realize that true contentment only comes from being rooted in God in the first place. Augustine said it best, "Our hearts are restless until they find rest in thee."

I have arrived at a place where my chief aim in life is just to walk daily in friendship with God. I don't want to be one of His kids who only goes to Him when I need something. My favorite times in prayer are the times when I am not praying about a need, but rather simply wanting to know Him and talk with Him. Although I love times of intense intercession that contend for breakthrough, my favorite type of prayer is to walk with the Father and ask Him what is on His heart and mind.

> We tend to drift from one disappointment to the next until we realize that true contentment only comes from being rooted in God in the first place.

As one who has grown in intimacy with God over the years, I now look back and ponder some of the strange things He has asked me to do as a result of some of our conversations together. Of the many things He has spoken to me about over the years, there are two things that are now starting to make sense to me. When He told me to do these two things, I honestly was not sure why, but in this current season of my life, they are starting to make sense.

The New Wine of Reformation

The first of the two things I want to share with you has to do with Azusa. As bizarre as this sounds, God told me to go to the location in California where the outpouring at Azusa happened, lick the ground, then come back and spit on the 40 acres where the church I pastor sits here in Greenville, South Carolina. Most of you reading this will know that Azusa is the place where, in the early 1900s, God poured Himself out in ways that we have rarely seen in church history. I had always wanted to visit Azusa, the site where God moved so mightily, but I can't say that I pictured myself licking the ground there. Yet I went, and there at Azusa, God planted something in me that would evolve into conversations that would end up in a prayer ministry ignited by Michael and Amber Thornton.

Michael is the author of the book *Fire in the Carolinas,* which tells the story of a lesser known minister named G.B. Cashwell who, during the time of Azusa, traveled to visit William Seymour to see for himself what God was doing. Cashwell was deeply impacted by his visit to Azusa. He came back to his town of Dunn, North Carolina, and it was there that God did extraordinary things similar to what He did at Azusa. As a matter of fact, Dunn, North Carolina was called "The Azusa of the East." Thousands upon thousands of lives were impacted by the outpouring of the Holy Spirit in Dunn during the early 20th century.

So what does this have to do with God telling me to go to Azusa? Well, Michael Thornton just happened to be at Azusa when I was there, although we never met. As a matter of fact, there was not even an event at the site of Azusa when Michael and I were there. We both just happened to be visiting the site on the same weekend, and what makes the story even crazier is that someone had handed me his book, *Fire in the Carolinas,* the week before I went to Azusa. To give a little more context to the visit, on the piece of ground where the great outpouring happened over 100 years ago there are now only office complexes. I licked the ground in front of a bunch of office buildings. Let me just say that obedience to God requires humility.

Upon returning home, I again did as God told me, spitting three times on the property of Bridgeway Church. Around this same time, I was discipling various leaders from around the country when someone got a word of knowledge that we should put tent pegs in the ground on the church's property. We did, not knowing that four years later God would lead us to put up a tent there as a house of prayer. God even sent two businessmen to provide the tent. We are now seeing God move in unusual ways in our faith community. It started with a spit that led to a tent that we believe will one day become a 24/7 house of prayer.

A few weeks after Michael and I were at Azusa, he felt led of the Lord to come and visit Bridgeway Church. While I was preaching that Sunday, in the Spirit I saw a flame of fire over Michael's head. Long story short, Michael is now on staff at Bridgeway. I sometimes wonder if I would have met him had I not gone to Azusa at the prompting of the Father. What the Father has done in bringing the two of us together is to unite prayer and the prophetic at Bridgeway. Prayer has become the bedrock of Bridgeway

Church where we are seeing the Father create a culture of habitation.

Why does any of this matter? Well, in this time of reformation in the church, I believe we will begin to see new partnerships, alliances, and relationships as God radically shifts His Bride. This emergence of new alliances is one of the ways to detect what the Father is doing. I have been prophesying a lot over the last three years that many leaders will be called to say goodbye to old relationships and partnerships as a result of the new wine God is pouring out.

> We are in one of those sovereign times in the history of the church when the Lord Jesus Christ divides brother against brother and sister against sister.

Many leaders I know can also feel the rumblings of change. This new wine of reformation cannot be stewarded by the same models and even the same relationships. God is actually widening the gap in His Charismatic stream of leadership where those who once identified themselves as very similar are now beginning to question where they stand on issues and even theological discernment. We are in one of those sovereign times in the history of the church when the Lord Jesus Christ divides brother against brother and sister against sister. When I look back on the very strange thing God asked me to do at Azusa while not giving me clarity as to why, I now understand what this act of obedience was all about.

The second thing the Father asked me to do, while giving me no prophetic inclination as to why, was to go walk the battlefields of Gettysburg, Pennsylvania. At that time in September of 2016, all I had was a handful of historical facts regarding Gettysburg and the Civil War.

Abraham Lincoln became president in 1860. His campaign was largely dominated by his intentions to abolish slavery across all states. Immediately after he became president, rumblings of discontent started in the South that resulted in seven Southern states seceding from the Union, thus forming the Confederate States of America. Upon the election of Abraham Lincoln, the country had split in two, one half composed of those states that opposed slavery and the other half of those who endorsed it. Months later, in the spring of 1861, the attack on Fort Sumter in the state of South Carolina served as the opening salvo of the war. Other states began to join the Confederacy, and before America could even get its bearings under a new administration, a civil war had broken out.

From July 1-3, 1863, a major battle in the Civil War in the United States of America was fought in the town of Gettysburg, Pennsylvania. Union and Confederate armies clashed in a tremendously bloody battle that saw the largest number of casualties of any battle during the Civil War. Many historians described the battle at Gettysburg as the turning point of the war. General Lee of the Confederate Army was determined to destroy the Union Army at Gettysburg, but the Union Army held their defense against surge after surge from the Confederate troops. Realizing that he had been defeated,

Lee took his army back into Virginia. The three-day battle at Gettysburg took the lives of thousands upon thousands of men and wounded thousands more, making it the costliest battle in the history of the United States. President Lincoln spoke at Gettysburg on November 19 of that year to honor the fallen soldiers. We remember that famous speech as the Gettysburg Address.

It is naïve to think that confronting something as nefarious as human slavery would happen peacefully. Historically this is not the narrative we find with mankind. Change of great magnitude never comes without immense cost.

> **Change of great magnitude never comes without immense cost.**

So why did God send me to walk the battlefields of Gettysburg? I think He wanted me to start wrestling with the aspect of confrontation. Confrontation is a part of the kingdom. Just look at the life and death of Jesus. The people Jesus came to die for didn't receive Him. They killed Him. We know that the Father is actually the One who led His own Son and our Savior to the cross, but let's not forget who called for the Lord's crucifixion. Simon Peter sure did not mind reminding the Sanhedrin who was responsible for the Lord's death when he confronted them (see Acts 4:1-22).

There are times in church history when we see a clash that pits brother against brother and sister against sister, and I believe we are in one of those times now. When Martin

Luther nailed his 95 Theses to that famous door in Wittenberg, Germany in 1517, all shalom did not rain down upon the church. What we got instead was the Protestant Reformation that split the church apart. Since then we have seen many divisions in the church over various theological issues. So who was behind the Protestant Reformation? Well, the short answer is that it was God. Yet why would God pour Himself out like that when He knew there would be so much disagreement and fallout from what He had Luther, Calvin, and the other fathers of the Protestant Reformation do? Sometimes, when the Father brings the sword of correction, it feels more like disagreement than peace.

In Charismatic circles, *Jezebel* is a term that is thrown around quite often when describing a controlling person. Yet when we look at Scripture we see that the real Jezebel in the Bible is a perfect case study for the coming conflict I see arising in the Spirit-filled stream of the church. In the book of Kings, Ahab was the king of Israel and he was married to a woman named Jezebel. Jezebel came from the lineage of a father who worshiped the god baal. She was not raised to fear the God of Israel, and that should have been Ahab's first clue that he was in for a rough path. Jezebel usurped her husband's authority when she served as the leader of Israel because her husband was too weak to not only lead God's people, but his own wife as well.

Jezebel is famous for scaring the mighty prophet Elijah by threatening to kill him. What's so amazing about this story is that Elijah had already called down fire on the prophets

of baal and showed outstanding courage and internal fortitude only to be driven away by the threat of Jezebel. This
woman Jezebel scared the man of God so badly that he fled
for his life. Elijah was not afraid of the showdown on Mount
Carmel, but he sure was terrified of one woman. This story
serves as a reminder to me that I am only one step away from
allowing the devil to use someone to scare me out of the
assignment on my life.

I never want to be a leader who runs from conflict no
matter how scary it is. For many of us, it is not the Father who
humbles us by removing us from our post; rather, it's we who
allow the devil to intimidate us to run from what we are actually anointed to handle. Most of the greats in the Bible faced
loud-mouth accusing enemies who wanted them defeated.
Take David, for instance. I think it was harder for him to
overcome his own brother Eliab and his spiritual father Saul
than Goliath. To expect that we are going to do great things
for and with God without opposition is quite silly.

> **To expect that we are going to
> do great things for and with God
> without opposition is quite silly.**

As we continue reading the story in Scripture, we find
that Jezebel finally met her match with a man named Jehu.
Jehu was the tenth king of Israel and had the typical sketchy
tenure as God's point person for the nation. Yet in one of
Jehu's bright moments, we see him doing what Elijah did

not have the courage to do. Jehu confronted Jezebel, and the story is quite dramatic. In Second Kings 9:30-10:36, we see Jehu go into the town where Jezebel was and have the eunuchs she was with toss her off a balcony. Not only was Jehu not intimidated by Jezebel, but he also did not waste any time ending her influence. This broken king was simply tired of an illegal leader playing any role in leading Israel astray. I have learned a lot from Elijah's failures in confronting and defeating Jezebel.

What does this have to do with the church today? I see God raising up people like Jehu who refuse to sit back and watch the church drift from the fear of the Lord into a false grace when so many are crying out for a sincere move of God on the earth. Before that move happens, though, major confrontation awaits and has already begun. I believe we will see many in the Charismatic stream in massive disagreement over theology. There is a rising conflict emerging and many people will pray for the enemy to stop stirring the waters when, in reality, it's the Lord Jesus Christ who is coming with a sword. Many of us misunderstand peace.

Chapter 4

MESSY HARVEST

For far too long, the church has been very quiet on issues that are causing people to stray further and further away from Jesus Himself. Right now, we see the Methodist Church and Presbyterian Church in an argument regarding homosexuality. There are strong voices on both sides of the fence, and it seems as though the divide will never be reconciled. In such times, God tends to be predictable. He always, and I mean *always* raises up Reformers. In fact, God has already begun to raise up voices who will remind us from a spiritual perspective what we saw Jehu do to Jezebel.

We may not be wrestling against flesh and blood, but I can promise you we are wrestling. That is why I teach on Ephesians 6:12 at least once every week at Bridgeway's Ascent University: *"For we wrestle not against flesh and blood, but against principalities, against powers, against the rulers of the darkness of this world, against spiritual wickedness in high places"* (KJV). I started Ascent because I refuse to be a leader who does not stand up and actually do something about what we see happening in the culture today. I am not going to sit back and do nothing while the educational system of America is now aggressively pushing an anti-Gospel agenda down our throats. It's happening at every level of education in this country. My question for church leaders in these times is, "Where are the Jehus who fear God more than Jezebel?" Where are the people who are willing to not only pray in the secret place about the issues that are causing people to stray from Jesus, but also speak against them and train others up to disagree with what the enemy is doing?

I value prayer so much that I have literally started a prayer initiative that I believe will eventually become a 24-hour prayer ministry on Bridgeway's property. Yet when I look at the story of Martin Luther and those Protestant Reformers, they did not stay in their prayer rooms. Luther's life was on the run for years after he nailed his 95 Theses to that door in Germany. The early disciples did not stay in that upper room after Pentecost. As a matter of fact, those early disciples were burned at the stake for a reason. While Nero unleashed his dogs upon the "lunatics" and burned them at the stake for threatening his powerful empire of Rome, the disciples (the Reformers) kept spreading the truth of Jesus and His kingdom in the face of fierce persecution.

I'm all for prayer and, believe me, we need that, but if we don't match the efforts of prayer with the actions of what Jehu did to Jezebel, then we may actually be creating cultures of disassociation while thinking we are battling in prayer. I love how Heidi Baker says that love has to look like something. I agree with that. Sometimes love looks like confrontation.

> **Love has to look like something. I agree with that. Sometimes love looks like confrontation.**

Within the Charismatic stream, confrontation will look like leaders not agreeing with other leaders and even preaching different realities. For this current reformation move of God, we will begin to see much more teaching on the fear of the Lord because the Father is correcting an overemphasis on the kindness of God that ignores His severity. Many will say that there is no such thing as hyper grace and that it's impossible to overemphasize God's kindness. Yet when you look at this through the entire biblical narrative, you see that it is very dangerous to present a partial truth. A partial truth played out for many years will lead people far away from the Father.

Paradox is what this reformation will look like, and those who are entrenched in the "kindness" camp will look at leaders like myself as being legalistic and harsh. When God begins to realign, He typically will send messengers who will be sharp and confrontational in order to redirect His church to where it needs to be. Reformation is not a comfortable thing. There is a Pauline initiative in the church right now where you will see spiritual fathers and mothers arise to realign misconceptions. Typically, this never goes over too well. God's prophets in the Bible rarely celebrated while they were playing their role to realign.

I see a bright future ahead for the Charismatic stream, but before that happens, I see a Gettysburg of disagreement and conflict. Those who were alive at the time of Azusa did not find the church at peace. When God raised up humble William Seymour, the church did not receive him at large. There were many, and I mean *many* divisions during the years God poured out His Holy Spirit in Los Angeles. Azusa was more like a Gettysburg at the time of the outpouring. Yet, as time passed, over 100 million people have reaped the benefit of what happened at Azusa.

The conflict I see emerging in the Spirit-filled stream is the Father's recipe to prepare His church for a massive end-time harvest. Right now, the team I lead is using manure to help the vegetables in our church garden grow so we can have a bountiful harvest to help feed the hungry. Sometimes a harvest simply needs a little manure. Typically, we want the harvest without the manure, without the mess.

> **We want the harvest without the manure, without the mess.**

Prophetic Chaos

In the summer of 2020, the Father told me to download Jeremiah Johnson's book *The Power of Consecration: A Prophetic Word to the Church.* Jeremiah is a well-known voice in the Charismatic stream who God has used like a lightning rod to expose where I believe the Charismatic stream now finds itself. I had never met Jeremiah and had never heard him preach, although I had a few people tell me that what I preach at Bridgeway often sounds a lot like what Jeremiah has been preaching.

I read Jeremiah's books and downloaded some blogs from previous years not knowing that the Father was about to connect us. To make a long story short, Jeremiah ended up coming to minister at Bridgeway Church. The first time I met Jeremiah, the Father told me many things about his ministry and the plans He had for this young man. As it turned out, Joe Biden defeated Donald Trump in the election. Small problem—Jeremiah, along with many other prophets, prophesied that Donald Trump would be reelected.

A few weeks after the election, and after many talks with my wife on what the Father was saying after the election, I decided to get into my truck one evening and drive and talk to God. I had a high level of passion in voicing my frustration with the Father that day because I simply wanted to know what He was saying. No prophet is my vine. I don't care if there are 300 prophets saying something as truth. If the Father does not say it is truth, then I want to be where the Father is on this or any other topic.

That day in my truck, I was not mad at God when I yelled out for Him to speak to me on the subject of why so many prophets were wrong about Donald Trump becoming president. I simply wanted to know what the Father was doing. Most of the time, the Father speaks to me through impressions because He so highly values faith. As far as I can tell from Scripture, faith is the highest form of currency in the Kingdom of God. Anyone who hears from God via impressions knows that faith is required to discern whether or not it is the Father speaking. Yet there are times for all of God's kids when the Father speaks so clearly that it does not take faith to discern what He is saying.

I was in my truck crying out to God that day because Jeremiah Johnson was scheduled to come and speak at Bridgeway, and as the lead pastor I wanted clarity from God as to whether or not I should have him speak. Why? Because I take very seriously who ministers at the place where I have been given jurisdiction and authority. I know that one day I will stand at the judgment seat of Jesus Christ and give an account of how I stewarded my assignment at Bridgeway. As soon as I asked the Father, this is what He said:

> Chad, I am humbling My prophets. I want you to reach out and tell Jeremiah you are with him and you support him. Over the coming months, you will see what I have been telling you about. My church will turn on each other. The prophetic stream is under My judgment right now. Notice the prophets who humble themselves and notice who does not. My judgment has begun.

I submitted this word to my wife and our closest community not knowing that the very next day Jeremiah Johnson would humble himself publicly to a much greater extent than any of the other prophets who missed it regarding the election. I felt an urgency to send him a text telling him that I was behind him and very proud of him. Why does this matter, and why am I even mentioning it here? Well, since that apology from Jeremiah Johnson and others in the prophetic, and the ensuing vitriol that came their way, the Father has exposed just how much the Charismatic stream needs reformation. The responses to Jeremiah and others who admitted their error were truly demonic. I have a hard time wrapping my mind around how so many people could be so deceived. Not only did many champion those prophets who missed it as not actually wrong, but they turned on those prophets who repented. Some prophets even received death threats. As the pastor of a local church with a long history of being Charismatic, I had never seen anything like this. Yet, hard as it was, there was also an element of encouragement for me because, for the longest time, the Father had been showing me the underbelly of the Spirit-filled stream and how He desires to heal it, and now I was seeing that underbelly for myself.

Building Bridges

I graduated from Beeson Divinity School in Birmingham, Alabama, a distinguished school that is known for its academic rigor, esteemed reputation for integrity, scholastic fortitude, and sound doctrine. Timothy George, Dean of Beeson School, is one of the most respected Reformed scholars in the world. I went to Beeson on the advice of Billy Graham. A friend of mine went to undergrad with Billy's grandson. We literally asked Dr. Graham where we should go, and he said Beeson. When Billy Graham gives you some advice, you better take it. So off to Beeson I went, not knowing what was right around the corner for me. After getting started in my marriage with Wendy and finishing seminary, I moved back to South Carolina and co-founded a ministry called Wayfarer. Our team did a lot of work with young people. Along the way God grew us and enabled us to help thousands through camps, conferences, and curriculum.

I traveled a lot and met thousands of people, mostly in the Baptist world, and enjoyed seeing God use me to help young people realize that He is real and wants to know them.

What I did not plan on happening was having an encounter with Jesus Christ and becoming a Charismatic. If you would have told me at Beeson that one day a guy named Darren Wilson would call me and ask me to be in two of his documentaries about God doing real things like healings, signs, and wonders in today's world, I would never have believed you. I was not opposed to the book of Acts in the Bible, but I honestly didn't think about it much.

> It's easier to dust for the fingerprints of God in your past than to discern what He's doing in your present.

A friend of mine once told me that it's easier to dust for the fingerprints of God in your past than to discern what He's doing in your present. That surely has been true for me. I grew up Baptist and went to a seminary with a strong Reformed core. Then God led me into the Charismatic world. Did I ever see that coming? No. Yet here I am now pastoring a church called Bridgeway. *Bridge.* About twenty years ago Andrew Wommack gave me a word of knowledge. "Charismatics are really going to hate you," he said. "You and your wife are a *bridge* and you have a global assignment." That was twenty years ago and thirteen years before my wife and I started Bridgeway Church. I was not even a charismatic at the time, and I had no idea what a word of knowledge was. Now here I am, a charismatic, writing a book about the rebuke at hand from the Father Himself. Hebrews 12:6 says:

"because the Lord disciplines the one he loves, and he chastens everyone he accepts as his son."

> ## The Father is a good father, and good fathers correct their own when they go astray.

I have heard hundreds of messages on the kindness of God over the past twenty years in the Charismatic stream, and I will forever be thankful for that. I can count on one hand how many messages I have heard on the severity of God in this same stream. I'm sure there are leaders out there who have been speaking on this reality, but I have not run across hardly anyone who has. In Romans, Paul writes, *"Notice how God is both kind and severe. He is severe toward those who disobeyed, but kind to you if you continue to trust in his kindness. But if you stop trusting, you also will be cut off"* (Rom. 11:22 NLT). The biblical definition of *severity* in this passage means "severity, roughness, rigor." Where did the severity of God go? Has God changed and now he is our Abba-Daddy who only calls the gold out in His beloved? The current reformation of His Spirit-filled stream will feel like heresy to many, and many will credit leaders like me as "being of the devil." Make no mistake about it, the Father is a good father, and good fathers correct their own when they go astray. The Charismatic stream is being disciplined by the Father because He's good. This message has nothing to do with legalism.

Is it possible that we have created a god in our own image and placed the title of "father" on him and gone on about our merry way only to now find that millions of Charismatics are waking up to the fact that perhaps God is a bit different than what they deemed Him to be? Five of the seven letters in the book of Revelation sure do seem to say that He is not always in a good mood. Jesus seems to be pretty upset at His church in five of those letters. Jesus Christ said, "*You are my friends if you do what I command*" (John 15:14). Obedience is a big indicator of friendship with God.

Before we see a move of God that we all so desperately want, we are going to see a cleansing move of God in the lives of His own leaders in the Charismatic church. It reminds me of the time when God would only allow the Zadok priests to minister before Him. He allowed other Levite priests to minister to the people, but as for the Zadok priests, they were the only ones allowed to minster to God Himself. We have seen leaders build altars around their own celebrity status even in small churches of fifty or less. We have seen ministers build altars around their own agendas and stages, with little to no accountability from fathers in the faith who are actually rooted in the local church. The Father is eradicating the celebrity spirit from the Charismatic stream. The fear of the Lord is returning to its rightful place. Keep an eye over the next ten years on those churches that build houses of prayer and focus on true biblical discipleship. God is dismantling not only the theology of the Charismatic church, but also its methodology.

Chapter 5

REBUKE

M ost of us flinch when we think about the word *crisis*. Crisis is defined as a time of intense difficulty, trouble, or danger, when a difficult or important decision must be made. I remember as a kid reading about the Black Plague and other diseases that swept through various parts of the world, but it all seemed so foreign and distant to me. Yet, as I write this, humankind is completing a full year of a worldwide pandemic that has put seven continents in a literal crisis. We are not fighting a bacteria that can typically be controlled by antibiotics. We are fighting a nefarious strain of coronavirus called 2019-nCoV.

I never dreamed I would see anything like this in my lifetime. This pandemic year has been a tremendously sobering time for the whole world. Despite all the advances in technology and medicine, we are seeing just how fragile life can be. In one moment, everything can change. Like most of you, over the past year I have had the opportunity to reflect on my own life and purpose, and I have sought God's perspective on the virus itself.

Here in the United States of America, we are seeing a political shaking that is perhaps unparalleled in American history. As a country, we have not been this divided since the days of the Civil War. The fallout from the tenure of Donald Trump as President and the passing of the baton to Joe Biden have been both deeply troubling and fascinating to watch. We are currently in a sort of gridlock almost like a scene out of a movie. Yet this is no movie. The turmoil is very real.

In the fall of 2020, as the presidential election drew near, the death of a man named George Floyd rocked the country. We saw hatred, fighting, violence, destruction, and protest on a level that reminded many of the protests and riots here in America during the time of the Vietnam War. During all of this I genuinely struggled to wrap my mind around some of the things I was seeing on the news. Positive COVID cases were surging, riots from racism issues were raging, and the upcoming presidential election had unleashed a level of ugly fervor that was sharply pitting us against one another.

I needed to talk to Father, so I went to my favorite place to connect with Him, which is my basement. There in my prayer closet I poured my heart out to Him like a hurt kid who just needed to hear from his dad. As I began to talk to Him about the crisis the world was in, He began to talk to me about the crisis in His own church.

There are times when we all get impressions from the Father, and then there are times when it is like a torrent of revelation from Heaven. There in my basement I began to get a torrent of revelation. In the culture of Bridgeway, like many other places, we call this "going into a prophetic swirl." The following is what I transcribed in my journal as the Father began to talk to me.

> The church is not going back to normal. As Luther was in Wittenberg, so are My Reformers who I am raising right now in their posts. Reformation is upon My church, Chad. This is real and it is now. I am riding the waves of this pandemic. The

return of My Son Jesus Christ is much closer than many people believe. All of Heaven knows that the time is drawing nigh. Before I pour Myself out in a way that many before you have prophesied, I am cleansing My church. I am dismantling My church and returning it to its roots before My Son returns. I am taking My church back to its roots. I am favoring you because you value what We [the triune God] value. You have passed many tests and you value discipleship the way in which My Son modeled and taught discipleship.

Many of My leaders today are like the priests I removed many years ago. I have had you teaching against the celebrity spirit for seven years for a reason. It is now time for the message you have been preaching to bear fruit. My judgment is upon My leaders who have gone the way of Balaam. My judgment is upon My ministers who have given in to this celebrity spirit. I am eradicating this from My church. You will begin to see houses of prayer replace houses of programs. Many of My leaders remind Me of Herod when he received praise from men instead of giving it to Me. I am humbling and removing leaders from My church who have drawn more people to themselves than to Me. Social media has become a snare for many of My leaders.

Your assignment is to rebuke and train leaders how to repent and walk away from this. People will believe that the pandemic is the reason that church is changing. The reason that church is changing is that I am the one behind the change. I am demolishing not only the celebrity spirit in My church, but also the model itself. When Luther pinned the 95 Theses to the wall on that fateful day, it was a theological reformation. You are about to witness a methodological reformation. I will elevate globally leaders who make disciples as true fathers and mothers who are not seeking their own stages. My Son will return on the wings of fathers and mothers creating cultures of discipleship in both the church and the marketplace. I am removing ministers and marketplace leaders who put their own agenda above Mine.

Your assignment, Chad, is to train others on how to know Me as their Father and then multiply that in the lives of normal people. Homes will become embassies in this final time before My Son's return. Churches that are known more for the popularity of a speaker will dwindle. The angelic will be attracted to places where fathers and mothers are raising up the next generation through the model of true discipleship. I am pruning My church and you will see much division between leaders within My own family. Many will attribute this to the devil, but only the discerning ones will understand that this is Me.

The church will never go back to the way it was. A marker of this will be to keep an eye on the places that put their number one priority on corporate prayer. You will help establish houses of prayer all over the Bible Belt first. I have given you access to the Bible Belt and you will train other leaders in how to do two things: pray and make disciples through a life-on-life model.

My judgment will be heavy in the Charismatic stream. I am elevating leaders that not many people know at this time. There is a changing of the guard in My leadership of the Charismatic stream globally. The marker of this new move is discipleship. I am removing leaders from their itinerant ministries and placing an emphasis on those leaders who do what I commanded in Matthew 28. Chad, keep making disciples and train My leaders how to make disciples.

This end-time move will see Me favoring marketplace leaders who turn their businesses over to Me by focusing on prayer and discipleship. Those who make disciples will see unexplainable favor on their lives.

I do not see the earth like many people think. I see the earth in quadrants. The brightest place on this earth from My perspective is Israel. Chad, bless Israel in every single time of intercession that you have. America is asleep, Chad, and I am waking My church up. I am riding on the wave of the chaos you see and feel. Reformation is at hand. Prepare to be hated by many of My own children who serve Me. There are many like you who I am raising to be a voice of this new reformation. I am dismantling the system and removing many of My leaders. You have now been given a Zadok invitation to minister before Me. Churches and businesses that exist to minister to Me first will see Me pour Myself out upon them. The valley to promotion in this reformation is the valley of Philippians 2. Go low, son, and stay low. Those who have gone high I will demote. Stay low, Chad.

After this prophetic swirl, I took three months to deeply ponder this word from the Father. Even though the prophetic has been a part of my life for twenty years now, and I have taught many people over the years how to hear God and act on what He is saying, there are times when the download is long and missional, and this was one of those times. I love words of knowledge, words of discernment, and prophecy, but downloads like these are like those we see in the Old Testament where God would give one of His prophets an alignment word for Israel.

As I reflected on what God had said to me, I wrote down two things that stood out to me and are helping me define and discern exactly what this current reformation is all about. The first thing that stood out to me is humility as we find it articulated in Philippians 2. This type of humility is a pathway to working out our salvation with fear and trembling. The second thing God highlighted is the elimination of the celebrity spirit via "Zadok" houses of prayer. Let's unpack each of these beginning with humility.

Crushing the Grapes

Abraham Lincoln once said that a man truly does not know who he is until he has been given a lot. He was right. Not too long ago I was with Heidi Baker and we were having a conversation about some of the things that I was going through at the time. The Father had given me a heads up that He was going to take me through a season of gossip and slander, but I had no idea that it would last so long and be so intense. Like most people, I have been through some difficult things in life, but going through a long season of accusation and public humiliation is not something I would ever sign up for.

> **A man truly does not know who he is until he has been given a lot.**

One month before a heavy season of gossip and slander was stirred up against my wife and me and Bridgeway Church, I began to have detailed dreams of the people who were stirring up the strife and how they would spread the attacks. These dreams became a reality and it was a great learning experience for me because God was faithful to show me things before they happened. And then the test of forgiveness came as God began to do a very deep work in my heart. I found myself developing a supernatural love and empathy for specific people who I knew hated me. I wish I could say that I learned what the Father was trying to teach me in a few weeks, but it was a long, difficult two-year journey into many conversations with God, my wife, and my community. Out of it all I began to realize that what God was doing in me was nothing more than a stripping. He was humbling me and teaching me to stop defending myself and trust Him.

The darkest night of that two-year journey was the night I begged God to let me resign from being the lead pastor of Bridgeway. I got on my knees and begged Him to simply allow me to do something in life without so much conflict. I hated the reality that so many people hated me, and I wanted to crawl in a hole and just pout about it. What I could not see at the time that I can see now is that God's way of crushing a leader is not the way many of us would choose.

I believe Paul's thorn in the flesh was the Judaizers who stirred up trouble for him wherever he went. Paul's ordained journey of humility came through the crucible of rejection, smear campaigns, lies, confrontation, gossip, slander, and hardship. Why would the Father intentionally choose this as the path for one of His greatest apostles of all time? Well, the Father is not like us. He loves to match the assignment of someone's life with the reality of a hard crushing. The degree of a person's assignment on the earth will always be matched by a significant crushing in God's kingdom.

The devil is not necessarily the one behind the crushing of a child of God. The Father Himself specializes in the process of crushing the grapes before He pours out the wine of His servants.

> **The Father Himself specializes in the process of crushing the grapes before He pours out the wine of His servants.**

Heidi once looked at me during this season of crushing and said, "Honey, going through what you are currently going through is not the hardest test. The hardest test will be when they all sing your praises." She was talking about developing a life of humility. A common theme throughout Scripture is that God hates pride and elevates and promotes humble people as demonstrated by Jesus Christ, who is the greatest example of humility the world has ever seen. Many of God's leaders in this time will find a significant season of crushing from the Father because at the heart of who He is, He simply values humility.

Jesus, our perfect King of the universe, lowered Himself and took the posture of a servant and went through what I call the "Valley of Philippians 2." Paul's epic description of what we are supposed to emulate is a sign for this current time of reformation for God's leaders in the marketplace and church. May Paul's words be a beacon of clarity in this time.

Therefore if you have any encouragement from being united with Christ, if any comfort from his love, if any common sharing in the Spirit, if any tenderness and compassion, then make my joy complete by being like-minded, having the same love, being one in spirit and of one mind. Do nothing out of selfish ambition or vain conceit. Rather, in humility value others above yourselves, not looking to your own interests but each of you to the interests of the others.

In your relationships with one another, have the same mindset as Christ Jesus: Who, being in very nature God, did not consider equality with God something to be used to his own advantage; rather, he made himself nothing by taking the very nature of a servant, being made in human likeness. And being found in appearance as a man, he humbled himself by becoming obedient to death—even death on a cross! Therefore God exalted him to the highest place and gave him the name that is above every name, that at the name of Jesus every knee should bow, in heaven and on earth and under the earth, and every tongue acknowledge that Jesus Christ is Lord, to the glory of God the Father (Philippians 2:1-11).

The current judgment at hand from the Father Himself is the humbling of His servants. To those who humble themselves, they will find the pathway of transformation painful yet rewarding. May we accept this grooming from the Father so that He can do the deep work inside of us, teaching us to love and forgive on a level higher than we could ever imagine.

The Zadok Purge

The second thing that the Father highlighted to me that day in my basement was the importance of ministering to Him first and foremost. This is something the church seems to have forgotten.

In Second Samuel 8 and First Chronicles 24 we find information on the lineage of the sons of Zadok. Zadok was a descendant of Eleazer, a son of Aaron the high priest. Ezekiel portrays the sons of Zadok as those who took a strong stand against the paganism that permeated their culture at the time. We also find in First Chronicles 16:39 that Zadok was leader of the priests serving the tabernacle of the Lord at Gibeon. Essentially, the Levites mediated the covenant of God with the nation of Israel in a representative capacity. As those who lived separate from the rest of Israel, these priests were to represent the level of holiness and purity God desired of His people. So what you had was a setup where God only allowed certain priests, Zadok priests, to minister to Himself while other priests were designated to minister to the people.

In the church specifically, we have seen an explosion of ministers who are addicted to ministering to people more than they are interested in ministering to the Lord Himself. Currently in both the marketplace and the church, we are seeing an invitation from the Father to those He has called to minister unto Him first and foremost. The writer of Acts says, "*As they ministered to the Lord and fasted, the Holy Spirit said, 'Now separate to Me Barnabas and Saul for the work to which I have called them'*" (Acts 13:2 NKJV). I believe this is a sign of the current reformation.

Have you ever thought about what it means to minister unto the Lord? How does a person do this? The story of the Zadok lineage gives us answers. In Ezekiel 44 we find some of the Levitical priesthood looking the part, yet in Ezekiel 8 God saw something in their hearts that He did not like. These priests were drawn to serve the people more than to serve God. Not only that, but some were idol worshipers who set up idols in the Temple. The judgment currently at hand from the Father is pointed at leaders inside His own kingdom, both in the marketplace and in the church, who look the part but are more drawn to the applause of man and the security of money and recognition than they are to simple and pure devotion to God Himself. They have set up idols and God does not like what He sees.

> This reformation at hand is about prioritizing Jesus Christ in all sectors of life.

There is a literal dismantling of businesses and ministries that carry the name of Jesus but do not carry the priority and focus on loving on Him and ministering to Him first. This reformation at hand is about prioritizing Jesus Christ in all sectors of life. There is a great purging currently going on in God's kingdom, and He is starting with His own leaders. This is the movement of those lowly and hungry leaders who care more about ministering to the Lord Jesus Christ than they do about making their next big sell or leading the next big thing in ministry.

The Zadok purge is upon us. Prayer tents will replace big stages. We will begin to see lead pastors turn their churches into houses of prayer and sprint to presence-based ministry to God first and then to people. Conferences that were once known to draw people around big, well-known names will be drowned out by prayer gatherings that spend hour upon hour pouring hearts out to simply magnify and worship Jesus Christ. He is jealous for our hearts. The presence and strength of God Himself, His glory, will return to the church, but there is much work to be done before that happens.

Chapter 6

IDOLATRY

've been on more diets than Oprah Winfrey. You name it and I have done it. I really bond with the people who've done the strange diets. I've done the low carb, medium carb, vegan, very low calorie, alternate day fasting, lettuce only diet, and many others. The funniest one I've ever done is the Cabbage Soup Diet. You buy a book for $12 called *The Cabbage Soup Diet* and then you proceed to eat nothing but cabbage soup until you lose 400 pounds and all desire to live. That's it. I have no idea how the cabbage idea came to be. It would probably be more successful if it were the chicken noodle soup diet because at least chicken noodle soup tastes good. I've even read some information about some type of volcanic ash supplement. I've read them all. When it comes to diets, I'm like Cliff Claven from the 1980s television sitcom *Cheers* who knew a little bit about everything. I know a lot about a lot of diets. I could probably write an article for *Harvard Review* about the Mediterranean Diet. Now I'm not going to be a vegan, ever, but I could probably go to one of their conferences and fit in perfectly. Minus the being fat part.

So why is dieting pertinent to our current discussion here? Well, on December 28, 2018, I had an encounter with God in my bathroom and it had to do with food. I've often wondered why God speaks to me so often in the bathroom and I think I have it figured out. I believe the bathroom is the most vulnerable room in the house and God does not have a problem encountering us in that space. First, God has no fear of encountering us anywhere. And second, when you think about it, we are all born naked in a state of vulnerability. As we grow up, we spend a good deal of time trying to cover our vulnerability with "fig leaves." If you struggle with vulnerability, then perhaps you have forgotten where you came from. You didn't come in a little tuxedo saying, "Hey everybody, I'm here!" Birth is messy and you have no clothes on, and the first thing you do is scream and cry.

> **God has no fear of encountering us anywhere.**

When I encountered God that day in December in my bathroom, I began to weep. I'm talking about one of those cries where you can't stop even when you try. My grandmother Mama Jane, who is now in Heaven, is my hero. I still have two of her chairs in my bedroom. I finally managed to get out of the shower and went and sat in Mama Jane's chair. With cell phone in hand I recorded what the Father was saying to me.

> Chad, I told you years ago that I would open up the nations to you when you gave Me your food. For the last twenty years, you have attempted diets in order to appease Me. You have seen your answer as a weight loss program. I do not see it that way. I see this as idolatry, and I will not release you into the nations to minister to the people in your assignment until you give Me your food.

Four years before this encounter, I had heard the same words. It was at Randy Clark's Voice of the Apostles conference in Nashville, Tennessee. Heidi Baker was preaching on stage and at one point she stopped and yelled, "The Father is coming for the Bible Belt." When she yelled that, the power of God hit me so hard in my stomach that I fell on the floor and began to shake. The shaking felt violent, and I heard God say to me, "I will give you access to the nations when you give Me your food." Little did I know that in the process of laying down the idol of food, God was going to show me the depths of His heart and His hatred for New Covenant idolatry.

As I began the painful process of giving Him my food, God developed a theology of suffering in me that I never expected. What God will typically do to get one of His children to lay down all idols is to take them through multiple grit-producing seasons of testing that refine us as though we are in a literal fire. Martin Luther changed the world from his revelation on Galatians regarding what happened at the cross, and yet he still struggled and wrestled with the book of James. There are many crucifixions we go through on the journey into the deep place in God's heart. Sadly, that's not the message you hear much anymore in the Spirit-filled stream of the church. What we do hear are too many voices that say that we will never have to go through any Gethsemane seasons in our lives because Jesus took care of that for us.

God still tests us, and many of His tests sure don't feel like grace. As a matter of fact, they can hurt so deeply that we question if we know Him at all. Any message of favor that negates the journey of sanctification through the pathway of suffering is not only unbiblical; it's demonic in origin. God did a deep pruning in Abraham, Noah, Simon Peter, Esther, Moses, Joshua, and even Jesus Himself. Yet when is the last time you heard someone in a Spirit-filled church preach on Genesis 12 and 22? There will be many teachers who will stand before the judgment seat of Christ and be held accountable before the Lord for leading millions of people astray with a false grace that promotes a well-being that looks more like therapy than it does the true Gospel of Jesus Christ.

Eugene Peterson said that the point of the spiritual life is death. Luke says, *"Whoever wants to be my disciple must deny themselves and take up their cross daily and follow me"* (Luke 9:23). Dietrich Bonhoeffer said, "When Christ calls a man, He bids him come and die." Where have all of the Bonhoeffers gone? We are seeing an invasion of messages in the Spirit-filled stream that present grace and favor in ways that bypass how God often chooses to groom those He loves dearly. These messages have turned millions of people into entitled, selfish, reward-seeking, soft, and easily offended Christians. What was once seen as fatherly guidance is now labeled as abuse. There is an explosion of teaching that makes Jesus Christ look more like a buddy than a Sovereign King who rules and reigns over the world with both kindness and severity.

I have yet to see someone highly elevated by the Father for kingdom work who has not first gone through a dark night of the soul. Many times, a leader in God's kingdom must go through multiple seasons that cut us so deeply that there is none of the old self left. Jesus Christ had to go through a desert temptation with the devil and was not allowed to eat food for 40 days, and yet many of the Lord's disciples don't believe that anything like this will ever happen to them in any way.

> There is an explosion of teaching that makes Jesus Christ look more like a buddy than a Sovereign King who rules and reigns over the world with both kindness and severity.

Idolatry is defined as extreme admiration, love, or reverence for something or someone. When I get my strength and comfort from anyone or anything other than God Himself, that is idolatry. There are many warnings in Scripture on idolatry. Second Timothy 3:1-2 says: *"But understand this: In the last days terrible times will come. For men will be lovers of themselves, lovers of money, boastful, arrogant, abusive, disobedient to their parents, ungrateful, unholy"* (BSB). Most of the time, God's kids look at idolatry as some foreign ancient Eastern concept that involves Asherah poles and other outdated practices that have nothing to do with the world in which we live. Yet a closer look at the Scriptures and the manifestation of Ephesians 1:17 (wisdom and revelation) we find that we may perhaps be in more idolatry now in the church than the world that Abraham lived in. Why is this such a big deal to God? In order to understand this, one must understand His jealous nature for his children. Exodus 20:5 says, *"You shall not bow down to them or serve them, for I the Lord your God am a jealous God, visiting the iniquity of the fathers on the children to the third and the fourth generation of those who hate me"* (ESV). Is it possible that God is actually furious over the amount of idolatry in the Spirit-filled stream that boasts of walking powerfully in the message of righteousness and power?

The Charismatic stream is in desperate need of a theology of suffering. Without it, this stream has become anemic and powerless in many ways simply because God's children are not willing to entertain the pathway of not only the apostle Paul, but of so many of our biblical heroes who have gone before us and walked in power. Jesus Christ had to go through Gethsemane on the way to the cross. Yet, for whatever reason, the Charismatic church seems to have drifted into a mindset that since Jesus went through Gethsemane, we will not have to. It is past time for us to slow down and ask the question, "Has idolatry invaded our lives in more ways than we think?" I have never met anyone in my life who is deceived who knows that they are deceived. Oh, how we don't know what we don't know.

After God spoke to me in the bathroom that day, I was about to find out just how much I was limiting God in my own life even though I had written two books on intimacy with God. I wish I could tell you that after my encounter with God at the Voice of the Apostles conference, I immediately changed and threw down the idol of food. I didn't. Humans have an amazing ability to rationalize, and I was one of them. I rationalized in my own mind that I could start exercising a lot and still eat what I wanted when I wanted and how I wanted. I began to hike up and down the mountains near the city where I live and made great headway in my physical fitness. And let me tell you, the mountains I hike are no joke. These hikes are very difficult and take four to five hours to complete.

The problem is that the Father didn't tell me to exercise when He warned me of my idol. He was clear with me when He said that my idol was food. He even had my best friend's wife call me with a word of knowledge regarding my idolatry of food. Her name is Lisa and I've known her my entire life. She called me and said, "Chad, I should have given you this word a while ago and I can't go any longer without giving it to you. The Lord says that you are having an affair." I was on an elliptical machine when she gave me the word and I immediately said, "Lisa, I'm not having an affair." She responded, "God says that you are having an affair with food." I have only been stung like that a few times in my life. I thanked her for the word and got really quiet in my soul as I wrestled with what God was telling me.

There are millions of people who have listened to messages on sonship and over time have somehow produced a posture in their hearts that has bastardized the message of grace to a place where the sin of idolatry and the message of Lordship are far from center stage. Jesus Christ never told us that we should "ask Him into our hearts." The call of Jesus Christ is to "follow Him." Only a few times in the Gospels does it talk about *believing Jesus*. The call in the Gospels is to *follow Jesus*. Those are two very different things. When a person truly follows Jesus, they find that this same Father who led Jesus through the testing of the desert and Gethsemane still takes followers of Jesus through extreme testing situations, not because something is wrong, but because something is right.

> **Jesus Christ never told us that we should "ask Him into our hearts." The call of Jesus Christ is to "follow Him."**

The pathway to a deep level in the Father's heart is through the backside of Philippians 3:10. The first part of that verse is what has been focused on for so long in the message of sonship, when Paul speaks of knowing Jesus intimately. Yet when we see how true bonding happens with God, we find it in the back part of that verse: "*I want to know Christ—yes, to know the power of his resurrection and participation in his sufferings, becoming like him in his death.*" Simon Peter was clear when he said:

> *Dear friends, do not be surprised at the fiery ordeal that has come on you to test you, as though something strange were happening to you. But rejoice inasmuch as you participate in the sufferings*

of Christ, so that you may be overjoyed when his glory is revealed (1 Peter 4:12-13).

In short, God is not bringing a new message to the stream that has seen so many people blessed by the message of sonship. It's an old message rooted in God Himself. The saints who ascend to the highest place on the mountain of God are those who go through the pathway of ordained and timely suffering. This is not suffering caused by the "big ole bad devil." Rather, it is seasons ordained by the Father Himself that burn us of what needs to be burned. There is a message of righteousness being preached that says indirectly that all suffering was taken care of at the cross, and all we have to do is understand and receive by faith our identity under the blood. What this does is bypass the role and method of sanctification in the life of God's children.

> **God wants His church back, and to that end He is dismantling His church to bring us a message that we need to hear.**

God wants His church back, and to that end He is dismantling His church to bring us a message that we need to hear. In the coming years we will see lead pastors close the doors of their churches to open them back up as houses of prayer that build an altar of prayer to minister before the Lord and to intercede for their city and region.

Jesus is leading many of His intimate followers to establish houses of prayer that have prayer and discipleship as their DNA. We will see God dismantling pulpits that have turned into stages for spiritual idols. He is dismantling churches that are built more around the personality and gift of the preacher-teacher and less around the presence of God. Green rooms will be replaced by prayer rooms. People with less musical talent but way more purity will begin to lead worship from these same stages. God is dismantling systems that on the outside look virtuous but on the inside carry a lack of God Himself.

It reminds me of when God did not want to name Saul the king of Israel because He Himself wanted to lead His people. Yet the people kept clamoring for a king, and God gave them what they wanted. We all know how that story went for Israel. Saul was a disaster as a king and God raised up a king who looked more like the heart of the Father. Just like in days past, today we will see God remove leaders of His church who look more like the House of Saul than they do the House of David because God wants His church back. He wants to be the focus of all attention. He is not happy that so many churches are being led by men and not by His own presence. In this end-time move of God, we will see a move toward consecration, holiness, and a desire to ascend God's mountain with pure hearts and clean hands.

Nazirite Time

Not too long ago, I felt a dread come upon me from the Lord Jesus Christ Himself. He had told me to go on a long fast from food, and I had talked myself out of it. I heard Him say to me, "You are at an impasse with Me, Chad," and indeed I was. I was at a gridlock with Him because of my idolatry of food and He was calling me out on it. Within minutes of hearing that word, I had someone walk up to me and give me a warning about food as an idol in my life. I started a long fast from food the next day, and the more I started to give to Him, the more He started to reveal to me. In fact, God started revealing things to me on such a high level that I was both stunned and deeply convicted.

Obedience is something that really matters to me, and I had chosen to "sort of" obey the warning word from the Father. I had eaten a little better and worked out a lot only to be reminded by Him that I was not being obedient. I was like King Saul when he was "sort of" obedient to God but chose not to fulfill everything God told him to do. Saul didn't kill the king God told him to kill, and it ended up costing him everything. His ninety-five percent obedience in God's eyes was actually one hundred percent disobedience because *he did not do what the Father told him to do*. It's one thing for me to sit here and preach what King Saul did not do, but when God began to open my eyes to the idolatry in my own life, I did not like what He was showing me.

We need to be careful what we call legalism because there are seasons that God will take us through that seem like we are striving when it's actually good old-fashioned consecration. Any Gospel message that does not cost me is in danger of being a deadly message because it takes out the role of our own consecration. My wife prays a prayer that goes like this: "Father, shine Your light, expose the truth, open our eyes, Holy Spirit help us." This is indeed a most dangerous and fruitful prayer. For those He chooses, there awaits a Nazirite season of consecration when idols die hard as God grooms His leaders in His kingdom. The Lord is coming back for a pure Bride, and as that time draws near, so will the demand on His leaders on the earth to be more consecrated than ever before.

The journey of confronting my idolatry with food would be the first of several. One night in the shower I had another encounter with God. "Chad," He said, "I want to teach you how to walk without crutches." I immediately thought, "Crutch*es* means there is more than one." The level of consecration must increase as we grow closer to the coming of the Lord Jesus Christ. What many of us believe are just pet sins or not even sin at all may actually be called idols in the mind of the Father. Any person or thing that we are gathering strength from other than the Father is evidence of idolatry. It will take a humble leader to not only let go of all idols, but to even admit that they have them in the first place. I know this to be true.

> It will take a humble leader to not only let go of all idols, but to even admit that they have them in the first place.

Chapter 7

THE JUDGMENT SEAT OF CHRIST

A few years ago, as I was reading through the book of Acts, I noticed that Paul mentioned something about the coming day of judgment. In Second Corinthians 5:10 he says, *"For we must all appear before the judgment seat of Christ, so that each of us may receive what is due us for the things done while in the body, whether good or bad."* This verse piqued my interest, and so I began to investigate the judgment seat of Christ. Hosea says that God's people die from lack of knowledge. How true this is, and that is why my bones burn to help people understand that whether or not any of us know it, all who are in Christ will literally stand before the Lord Jesus Christ one day to give an account of his or her life. This face-to-face moment is known as the judgment seat of Christ.

For three years, I studied this reality intensely and was deeply impacted by what I found. Yet I had not heard one single sermon preached on the reality of the judgment seat of Christ—until recently. Again, I'm sure there are teachers out there who are teaching on this subject, but as a pastor of a Charismatic church, I have had very few conversations on this topic.

It is an awkward thing for the God of the universe to confront you on something that is standing in the way of your walk with Him. Thankfully, He confronted me on my idol. The idol of food in my life was standing in the way of my walk with the Father. It took His conviction piercing my life, along with a serious dose of the reality of the judgment seat of Christ, to propel me into action. My biggest goal in life now is to finish well at the judgment seat of Jesus and cross that finish line with purity and a life well lived.

One day at a staff meeting at Bridgeway, we were discussing Second Corinthians 5:10 followed by a short video teaching about the concept of the judgment seat of Christ when John Helms, one of my best friends, literally yelled out loud, "Why has no one ever told me about this?" John and I went to seminary together and have walked in friendship for over twenty years. It startled me when he yelled. It was not a funny moment where he was looking to make someone laugh. John has a master of divinity degree and has been in vocational ministry for a long time, yet he was ignorant on this subject.

> **The enemy has given the church in the West a sleeping pill.**

I have been in ministry for a long time, spoken in lots of places, and learned from many incredible leaders, but this has never been a topic of discussion in my circles. For me personally, besides John Bevere and Mike Bickle, I have never heard anyone preach or teach on this subject. Why? Why are so many Charismatics turned off by what Paul is talking about in Second Corinthians 5:10? When is the last time you heard a sermon preached on the judgment seat of Christ? Better yet, how familiar are you with this topic from Scripture? I think the aspect of standing before Christ and being accountable for our actions in life is a fuzzy and even foreign concept at best to many Christians. I personally believe that the enemy has given the church in the West a sleeping pill, and many if not most of God's leaders in the church and the marketplace literally never even think about the judgment seat of Christ.

Many in the Spirit-filled stream of the church have forsaken the local church in favor of podcasts. They refuse to serve a local house and submit to any form of leadership because they don't want to be "controlled." And even if they were to serve in a church, it is very likely they would never hear a sermon preached on the judgment seat of Christ. How sad.

"Won't Back Down"

In the book of Acts, Paul gets arrested in Jerusalem for preaching about Jesus Christ (see Acts 23:35). Some people even want to kill him. Paul is taken to Antonius Felix who is to decide Paul's fate (see Acts 23:23-24). Antonius Felix is an interesting guy. He was known for being harsh and selfish and was not a good man. He went from being a slave to a governor after being promoted by Caesar.

Paul ends up meeting with Felix, some Jewish elders, and some other people, and in typical fashion they talk about how much trouble Paul is causing them. Paul denies any wrongdoing and Felix suspends the conversation until some other people can arrive to hear the accusations. Paul writes:

> *After some days Felix came with his wife Drusilla, who was Jewish, and he sent for Paul and heard*

him speak about faith in Christ Jesus. And as he [Paul] reasoned about righteousness and self-control and the coming judgment, Felix was alarmed and said, "Go away for the present. When I get an opportunity I will summon you" (Acts 24:24-25 ESV).

Felix must have been either convicted by the Holy Spirit or simply intrigued because he and his wife wanted to hear more from Paul.

The apostle Paul is one of my heroes and I can't wait to meet him one day. He was ruthless in his boldness for the Lord Jesus. He reminds me of that Tom Petty song "Won't Back Down." I often laugh and say that Paul would probably have a church of less than ten people in America today. If a leader in today's church had a moment to share the Gospel of Jesus Christ with a governor, I seriously doubt that he would share about the "coming judgment."

> **Paul would probably have a church of less than ten people in America today.**

Paul had one shot to share the Gospel with Felix and he did not say, "God wants to be your Abba Daddy. If you will simply believe in Jesus, then the Father will then train you to see yourself as clean as Jesus Christ, and He will only convict you of who you are in Christ. He is pure love and He will only train you to see the gold in yourself." Not only did Paul not say this, but he actually talked to Felix about self-control and the coming judgment. Perhaps Paul got a word of knowledge about Felix, because history tells us that Felix actually took another man's wife as his own. The woman standing in front of Paul was actually stolen by Felix from another man.

In today's church, Paul would be called an abuser for even saying such a harsh thing to Felix. I think that even Jehu would be kicked out of the 21st-century church for throwing Jezebel down from that balcony. The apostle Paul shared the message of God with Felix and it made Felix so uncomfortable that he said, "Um, I'll get back with you when I can."

A Man in Need of God's Truth

When I first got revelation on this story from Acts, I was surprised and immediately began to ask the Father about this. That was a few years ago, and since then I have thought thoroughly about this passage and its implications. My question was and is, "Where are the leaders who are talking about this, who are actually sharing the Gospel?" The main message I have heard for twenty years in the Spirit-filled stream is all about the kindness of God and how that is what truly changes people. Hang on a second here. I love Romans 2:4 as much as the next person, and the Father is truly the nicest person I have ever met, but have you ever read one verse further? Romans 2:5 says, *"But because of your stubbornness and your unrepentant heart, you are storing up wrath against yourself for the day of God's wrath, when his righteous judgment will be revealed."* Whoa!

Is it possible that we have created a message of the kingdom that is not an accurate representation of the real Kingdom of God? Yes, Jesus loves me, and He is also a literal king who will literally judge my life one day. I have not had a single day pass in the last few years that I don't think about this. Some may call this legalism, but I call it truth. Yes, Jesus Christ is grace, but He is also truth (see John 1:14). There are some fifty passages in Scripture where Jesus points toward eternal rewards. In fact, He was so blunt that it's hard to misunderstand the importance of what He is saying.

The salvific story of God in the Bible according to Paul looks way more paradoxical than many of us have grown up learning. For example, Paul tends to say that we are saved and yet we are being saved. He speaks often about finishing the race and fighting the good fight so we don't lose crowns or prizes. On almost every page of Paul's letters I found myself getting angry at what I did not know. Does the Father love me? Yes, and as a matter of fact, I am overwhelmed with how much He loves me because of the blood of His own Son. But my point is that many of us are also not aware that what we do on this earth with Jesus has a large say in what we will be doing for all eternity. Is that because we are not reading the Bible to see what it actually says? One of the wisest and boldest things we can do as disciples of Jesus is to get our theology directly from the Word of God and not some other person who has interpreted the Scriptures for us.

A few years ago, I was in Amelia Island, Florida, walking on the beach when God said to me:

Chad, you will be rewarded based upon the obedience to the assignment I have given you. You will have opposition all the way to the judgment seat, but the only person that can remove you from your post is you. I will take care of any person who opposes your obedience to your assignment. You will have massive opposition to the degree of your obedience to Me. Have no other gods before Me. I am going to show you the fear of man in your heart and deliver you from idolatry.

> **Holiness and obedience matter now and they will matter on judgment day.**

Let me be clear here—we all will stand before the Lord Jesus Christ on that great and dreadful day, and each one of us will be held accountable for what we have done with the assignment He has given us. The way in which we live our lives matters. Holiness and obedience matter now and they will matter on judgment day. I am so thankful to God for opening my eyes to this truth. I am a man in need of God's truth.

Perverted grace says that the Gospel does not cost us anything but a simple "yes to Jesus." The true biblical Gospel will cost each of us everything. Scripture shows us that the closer Jesus got to the cross, the fewer disciples He had. In fact, Jesus went through many "crucifixions" before

His ultimate crucifixion. We are made clean by the cross of Christ, but that isn't a license to live as we wish. The message of the Gospel of Jesus Christ is that not only am I now clean, but I must now forsake all other lovers in my life in order to walk with Him. I need to ask each one of you: Where are you in your Gospel walk with Jesus? Is the burning desire of your heart to please your Master more than anyone or anything in your life? Are you willing to allow God to lead you through a tough, gritty season that releases you into the pathway of Paul, Moses, Abraham, Esther, and so many others who chose to follow the narrow road? Are you willing to allow God to introduce you to the pathway of suffering that produces a grit in you that can help you finish well all the way to the judgment seat?

The Spirit-filled stream has been lulled to sleep by the devil and God is now raising up voices to scream at the Bride, "WAKE UP!"

We are desperately in need of a theology of suffering that has absolutely nothing to do with sickness. When Jesus calls a person to follow Him, He bids that person to come and die. He says it quite clearly in Luke 9:23: *"Then he said to them all: 'Whoever wants to be my disciple must deny themselves and take up their cross daily and follow me.'"*

The Necessity of Obedience

One of the most refreshing things I have learned about the judgment seat of Christ is that it has nothing to do with whether or not I will be with God for all eternity. Salvation is in Jesus Christ alone. When I gave my life to Jesus in 1984, I became His disciple. If I had died right then in 1984, I would be spending all eternity with God. Through the Scriptures, God has shown me that the judgment seat, which in Greek is best translated as the "reward seat," is about what I have done with my obedience to what He has called me to do. Jesus Christ Himself said, "You are My friends if you do what I command." The call to obedience in the Christian life is a necessity.

> **For Jesus, to hear God is to obey God.**

People have left Bridgeway Church over the years for the same reason I have heard time and time again, which is, "Chad focuses too much on obedience and not the grace of God." The only fruit of friendship with God is obedience. This sounds like legalism to so many in the stream in which I pastor. I believe it's because we have seen so many thousands of messages on identity and sonship over the last 30 years in this stream that we have drifted from the biblical roots of obedience. Jesus Christ would have prayed the Shema, the oldest Hebraic prayer in Jewish history, every day twice a day without fail. The Hebrew word *shema* means to hear and obey. In Hebrew, you literally can't separate the idea of hearing and obeying God. For Jesus, to hear God is to obey God. So many Charismatics have focused on the hearing part but have taken away the idea of obeying God. God has not changed His nature since Samuel told Saul, "*To obey is better than sacrifice*" (1 Sam. 15:22).

At the judgment seat of Christ, my sins will not be in question because that was dealt with at Calvary. By accepting the blood of Jesus Christ over my life, I am not only forgiven now, but my sins will not be on my record on that day of judgment. Thank God Almighty that this is the scenario, but what many—and I mean many—of God's children fail to realize is that what you do with your life in obedience to Jesus Christ after your decision to give your life to Christ will be of utmost importance on that day of judgment. Our life lived with Christ here on this earth is an internship for what we will be doing for all eternity.

Finishing Well

When I began to live my life through the lens of this "internship," I quickly adapted to a more focused view of who God is, what He's calling me to do, and how quickly I respond to Him. He has given me a burden that burns in my bones to warn His Bride of what lies ahead. The message of hyper grace takes His love to such a level that we now have a generation of people who have zero concept that they will be held accountable for their own obedience or disobedience to what the Lord Jesus Christ commanded for them to do. Not only is Jesus not my buddy, He's also not passing out suggestions for what I should or should not do. His commandments are real, and there are consequences to my own obedience on the earth.

If God's kids would wake up and understand the reality of the judgment seat of Christ, it would give us sobriety in a matter of seconds. For me, the judgment seat is about a matter of perspective. Just thinking about it has given me a grit and tenacity that I have never carried before. Who cares how many times someone comes against what God has for you to do on the earth? They will not be standing there on your day of judgment. Does it really matter in the grand scheme of things how many accusations come against you during your time on the earth if you realize that there will not be one single accuser who stands against you on that day of judgment?

As a lead pastor, I have heard just about everything under the sun in terms of accusations from others and their own disappointment in who I am and who I am not. As I have processed how to lead in the face of opposition, I always fall back onto the fact that in the present and in the end, there is only one single person's judgment that matters to me. It is incredibly freeing to be delivered of the desire to please anyone except Jesus Christ. Now I know why Paul talks so often about not losing the prize and finishing well.

I hear people say that they are not that worried about what Heaven looks like in terms of rewards as long as they are with Jesus. While this may sound spiritual and projects a sense of contentment, the problem with this thinking is that it is opposed to Scripture. There are numerous passages and verses of Scripture that reference rewards and the reality that what we do on this earth affects what we will be doing in Heaven (see Rom. 14:10; Acts 25:22; 2 Cor. 5:10; Ps. 62:12; Matt. 16:27; 1 Cor. 3:10-15; 4:2; 2 John 8; Luke 19:17-19). The overemphasis on our identity in Jesus Christ has lead millions of God's children away from the reality of Scripture itself. Disobedience is costly and deadly even in the current age of grace. It borders on universalism, which should frighten you. It goes something like this: 1) God is love; 2) all I need to do is receive God's love; 3) my main job is to remain in love and learn how to love; 4) God is tender and will not call out any deficiency or blind spots in my life; and 5) learning to love is why I'm here and those who don't do this simply have not found the God of the Bible yet.

> **Disobedience is costly and deadly even in the current age of grace.**

If you are not familiar with universalism, it is the belief in universal salvation—that *all* will be saved. That is not what the Bible says. In John 3:16, it says that **all who believe in Jesus Christ** "*shall not perish but have eternal life.*"

The Charismatic stream is being called to accountability by the Father for giving so many people an inaccurate picture of God. There is so much truth in what I am sharing, yet without any revelation of the fear of the Lord and the consequences of our own disobedience we will continue to drift into the land of making Jesus our buddy while forgetting that He is the Sovereign King who judges now and will judge each one of us when you and I stand before Him one day.

As a pastor, I have seen how the devil uses true statements to get a child of God slowly drifting off onto a deadly path by disguising himself as an angel of light. Over and over I have seen the devil use the idea of love and unity to his own evil advantage. Misrepresenting God is what satan specializes in the most. His entire existence is all about misrepresenting the Father. Satan has hated God from the beginning, even before humans were created. It makes perfect sense to me that Jesus was manifested to reveal the Father, and therefore satan exists to misrepresent the Father. When satan realized that he could not defeat the message of the kindness of God that exploded onto the church scene in the last 50 years, he simply joined it.

In this age of grace I see so many new teachers coming on the scene and acting as though they have discovered things about grace that have never been uncovered in 2,000 years since the resurrection of Jesus Christ. Where are the teachers who are emphasizing the importance of our obedience to the Lord's commandments? We need to wake up and realize that there is an immediate judgment at hand that has to do with the overemphasis on the kindness of God at the expense of His sovereign severity. There is a terrifying side to God that is rarely talked about anymore. At the end of his life, Solomon said it better than I can: "*Now all has been heard; here is the conclusion of the matter: Fear God and keep his commandments, for this is the duty of all mankind*" (Eccl. 12:13).

You will have a very difficult time finding a Charismatic who is open to the fact that not only does God love His children, but He will also oppose us as well. There are so many who describe the season they are in as a "wilderness that is alluring them to a deeper place in the Father's love," only to discover that it's actually a season of humility as a result of the Father opposing their own pride. Many quote passages of the Father's love while they are actually experiencing the Father's rebuke. Many of us who are in the Spirit-filled stream believe that we are in seasons of spiritual warfare when what we are experiencing is actually opposition from the Father.

> Many quote passages of the Father's love while they are actually experiencing the Father's rebuke.

The kindness of God saved my life and I've not gotten over it and I hope I never do. But He has taken me on a journey of understanding His severity as well. If we are growing in our identity in Christ but there is no evidence of submission and obedience to the Father in the same way that Jesus was submitted to Him, then we need to honestly ask ourselves some serious questions.

We have been lulled to sleep with a Disney-like message of the Gospel instead of teaching what Paul taught about the coming judgment of Jesus. The messages Jesus gave John as he sat on the Isle of Patmos are shocking when you understand what those messages actually say. Does Jesus seem like He was in a good mood in those letters? (Read Revelation

2–3.) Go be a Berean and read them for yourselves (see Acts 17:11). Not only is He not in a good mood but Jesus is actually giving a warning to the church He died for. Jesus is coming again, and He is raising up end-time messengers to warn the church of His coming judgment. In fact, He woke me up in the middle of the night one night to tell me that there are millions in His church who think they are regenerated but are not. As a pastor who cares deeply for the flock, it shook me. God help us! Open our eyes, Lord!

Recently, I was reflecting on how much opposition Nehemiah had to the wall that God ordained for him to build. At every turn, it seemed like Nehemiah's own people were a constant distraction for him. The accusations never seemed to stop. Yet Nehemiah pressed through and did what God told him to do. Paul did the same thing with the Judaizers who heckled him relentlessly. What I have found to be true as a Jesus follower is that most of the opposition that you will face in your life will come from people right around you who love the same Jesus you do. Yet there is an unfair advantage to being driven by the judgment seat of Christ because you will learn to barely even hear what tends to take most people down.

David had to overcome his own family in order to take down Goliath. Jesus had to overcome His family of naysayers. I can't imagine enduring a tenth of what Paul had to go through on his way through his assignment, but I can without a doubt say that Paul found focus in knowing what lay ahead at the judgment.

Don't be a Felix and tell the Lord that you will "think about this later at a more appropriate time." Get focused now and set your compass to the day that the New Testament says is waiting for you. Instead of dreading what the judgment seat may look like for you, why don't you study it for yourself and align your life appropriately? If you will do this, you will find a vigor and passion to finish well even though you may go through much opposition to what the Father has assigned you.

Is God kind? Yes, He is the kindest person I've ever known. And He also waits to judge my life one day. This paradox keeps me sober, hungry, and focused. Perhaps it can do the same for you as well.

Chapter 8

THE FORGOTTEN COMMANDMENT

When I was two years old, my dad put a golf club in my hands. I have memories very early on of walking around the house with my driver in my hand feeling like a real man who was a warrior at heart. I had no idea what golf was, but I loved walking around with that club. As I grew up, I found my identity in golf. In fact, golf is the sport that bonded me with my dad, grandfather, brother, and many friends. I don't recall a time when golf has not played some sort of role in my personal development. I played through school, went to college on a golf scholarship, got my first job in ministry as a result of playing good golf with a lead pastor of a church I would end up serving, and now I play often with people in my own church. My oldest son is headed off to college to play golf. It seems like God has ordained this sport to play more than one purpose in my life.

Five years ago, my son Sam had his first professional lesson. I had no idea how much of a setup this was going to be. His instructor was Bradley Hughes. We didn't know that Bradley would quickly become one of the most sought-after golf instructors in the world. He played pro golf and had an impressive career, and when that career ended he took up teaching the game. There are many teachers in golf, but very few have the credentials that Bradley carries. Currently, if you Google his name, you will find that lots of current PGA tour players come to Bradley for coaching. Over the last few years, I can't tell you how many times Sam has texted me and let me know that a pro is on our club's driving range and that Bradley is working with him. For our little golf course here in South Carolina, it's a pretty big deal to show up and find a globally known golf name on our range working with our coach.

As I have gotten older, I have found that I love coaching golf even more than I do playing golf. Golf is the kind of game that can be complicated and frustrating for many people. To improve my coaching and playing skills, I look for opportunities to shadow Bradley when he is giving lessons. The closer I get to the teaching tips from this grade A professional coach, the more I realize that he teaches the fundamentals of the game that have been around since its inception. He'll show clips of some of the all-time greats who have been gone for many years. He'll talk about Bobby Jones' techniques, and what Ben Hogan did at impact to hit the ball. Great golfers typically don't come up with new swing styles that have never been invented. Instead, they do what the all-time greats did many years ago. Technology may change, and there are young whippersnappers who try new things, but the current great ones do what the great ones of old did many years ago, especially at impact. It's not about the new, but about developing an appreciation for the nuances of what is timeless.

I've never seen two people have the same golf swing. We are all so unique, different, quirky. And that is true of all aspects of the life of each one of us. Yet despite our differences, we all seem to be searching in our heart of hearts for the answers to two fundamental questions: 1) "Who am I?" and 2) "Why am I here?" Many people are searching to find what it is that God wants from them in life, not knowing that

His desire and, dare I say, *commandment* is found in Matthew 28:19: "*Therefore, go and make disciples of all the nations, baptizing them in the name of the Father and the Son and the Holy Spirit*" (NLT). How it is that so few people actually do what Jesus Christ commanded us to do in this verse? I really began to seriously seek the ins and outs of my own faith around the age of thirty-five. I wanted to know why I believed what I believed. I wanted to better understand the "how" of Jesus. What did He do and how did He do it?

How Did All This Happen?

It is safe to say that I pursue the ins and outs of Christianity with some of the same methods that I pursue my golf swing, just with much greater purpose and intensity. I start out asking a lot of "how" questions of the Lord, theological questions that have resided in my heart and mind most of my life, questions like who God is and what is He like. For example, have you ever asked yourself how Christianity overtook Rome within 350 years of the resurrection of Jesus Christ? They had no printing press, mass gatherings, social media, conferences, television, or any of the other outlets that we have had over the years. We all likely agree on the "why" questions—this is about Jesus Christ and His kingdom. My question is, "*How* in the world did we, the church, get to where we are today, and *how* has the seed of Jesus' life multiplied into what we are currently?"

The Father placed Jesus Christ at the base of perhaps the most tyrannical empire the world has ever known. Take a moment to think through the time and place where God placed His Son. It was a far cry from what the earth was like when God walked with Adam and Eve in the Garden of Eden. To fully appreciate God and His ways, we must understand the world Jesus was born into. The King of kings and Lord of lords made His grand entrance through Bethlehem at the base of a sick, twisted, tyrannical, and oppressive Roman regime that towered above little Israel. The fact that Rome was declared a Christian nation within a few hundred years after the Lord ascended is to me rather mind blowing.

> The King of kings and Lord of lords made His grand entrance through Bethlehem at the base of a sick, twisted, tyrannical, and oppressive Roman regime that towered above little Israel.

But in the early days after the Lord's ascension, Rome was not a fan of any person who had put their faith in this dead Nazarene named Jesus. At least that's how Rome saw things. If you read *Foxe's Book of Martyrs,* you will see very clearly that Nero tried his best to snuff out the early church of Jesus Christ of Nazareth by unleashing his dogs upon Christians and burning them on stakes with iron rods sometimes going through their bodies. The term *Christian* was a derogatory name given to Christians by the Romans, not a term of endearment. Christians were pests to the mighty Romans. Yet as history shows us, the Romans could not put out the fire of God in the fledgling church of Jesus Christ no matter how hard they tried. The mightiest nation on earth at the time was powerless against the church of Jesus Christ. When Rome finally figured out that they couldn't beat the church, they joined it. In the history of the church, no political, economic, or ideological framework has been able to extinguish Christianity since the moment Jesus Christ laid down His life on the cross.

So, how did all this happen? Is there any biblical precedent for the way in which church is done? If Jesus Christ were in my shoes as a pastor of a church in 2021, what would He do? Would He spend most of His time preparing for one sermon a week and perhaps visit a few people? If He were in the marketplace, would He spend His time selling a product and attempting to be productive and successful? Would Jesus do what most people do if He were on the earth now? One day I simply asked Him. I said, "Lord, what would You do if You were pastoring a church?" His answer was simple and profound. He said, "I would make disciples."

The Mandate of Multiplication

Discipleship is God's recipe to multiply His culture on the earth today. It is not some new idea. It is an old commandment that has been neglected by the church for far too long, and it flies in the face of the celebrity spirit that we see infiltrating the church today. Methodology is important to God, and this reformation of the church will predominantly be found in the "how" of practical Christianity. Those who make disciples the way God says is *His* way will thrive, and those who do not will not. The Father is taking His church back to its roots, and any spiritual leader who opposes Heaven's ordained, fundamental reality of discipleship will find the God they love actually opposing them. The church is not being overrun by the devil. It is, however, being dismantled by the Father. He is restoring the foundation of what has been His normal since the beginning. We have drifted from the original plan that Jesus Christ intends for His Bride.

> He is restoring the foundation of what has been His normal since the beginning. We have drifted from the original plan that Jesus Christ intends for His Bride.

Let's go back to the Garden of Eden for a moment. The vast majority of Charismatic books I have read concerning the Garden of Eden either deal with theology or ideology. For instance, we discovered through Paul and his writings that Jesus came to the earth to purchase back the authority that satan took from Adam and Eve. As a result, we can now extend the kingdom of Heaven onto the earth through the authority that belongs to those who are in Christ. Much of our authority comes through our own faith-filled words. Time and again I have seen my own words influence physical sickness as I command someone's body to line up under the mandate of Heaven. I have seen weather patterns shift as a result of authority prayer, people's bodies healed, and extremely accurate prophetic words given. I not only theoretically believe in the authority that Jesus purchased back for us, but I actually see it as well.

I have preached many sermons on how we are called to rule and reign on earth because that is what we saw Adam and Eve doing in Genesis 3 before the fall. Although I am so very grateful for what I have learned from so many pioneers of the faith who have gone before me, I must ask: "Why are there so few books and teachings in the Charismatic stream on the glaringly obvious mandate of multiplication that we read about in the Garden?" And why are we watering down the mandate "go make disciples" to our current-day mass gatherings, online podcasts, and published books, all of which you can do without even knowing someone's name? How is that the kind of discipleship that Jesus lived and modeled? Let me explain.

When you read the narrative of the Garden in Genesis, it is obvious that God is creative—that He is *the* Creator. And to say that He is an artist is an understatement. He comes from Himself, has no beginning, and speaks things into existence. Throughout Scripture, God seems to be driven by connection. Right from the start we see this in Genesis 1:26 where it says, "Let us make man in our own image." God was in this garden, and from the dirt He created a man whom He named Adam. I have spent many hours just reflecting on what that must have been like. What did Adam feel when his eyes popped open and he looked into the face of the One who created him? Was he overcome with love, acceptance, connection, and peace? I think perhaps Adam felt whole, safe, and in awe of not only God Himself, but of his surroundings.

We know from Psalm 82 that even before Adam was created, there was a council around God—a community, if you will, of Heavenly beings. After Adam was created, God then created Eve from Adam's rib. What an amazing connection there must have been between Adam and Eve. And just imagine what it must have been like for Adam and Eve to be connected to one another while also connected to God.

God wrapped Himself in flesh and came to the earth in the person of Jesus, who grew in His earthly body even as He grew in His intimacy with Abba. Then, in His 30s, the first thing Jesus did when He began His ministry was to pray all night—to be in conversation with His Father before He picked His family of disciples to connect with and to do life with. Why did Jesus want disciples? Did He simply want community? Did He need some new adult friends? No. He knew that in order to expand Heaven's jurisdiction on the earth, He needed to *model* and *teach* and *do life* with people for a deliberate time so they, too, could learn and be in a position to teach and model Him to others. In the Jewish culture of Jesus' time, that kind of intimate connection with followers was the norm. It was the way of rabbis.

Jesus didn't choose a wide range of people to simply evangelize and convince of who He was and then give them an opportunity to believe it so He could check-mark the box labeled "multiplication." Nor did He refer to the crowds who gathered to hear him as His "disciples." He inquired of Abba regarding who He needed to invest in with an intimate life-on-life relationship so that He could expand Abba's kingdom,

His ways, His whys, and His hows. And while it is clear from Scripture that some sow, some water, and some see the harvest, Jesus' mandate is also clear—*each* of us are to be about making disciples. Jesus' method must be our method in this modern day if we are to be true followers of Him. Jesus in the Gospels is the same as He was in Genesis 1 and 2. God, who is the same yesterday, today, and forever, did, does, and always will value connection and multiplication.

> He inquired of Abba regarding who He needed to invest in with an intimate life-on-life relationship so that He could expand Abba's kingdom, His ways, His whys, and His hows.

Once Adam and Eve were created, God told them to go and multiply. His intention was to be with them as family. The natural by-product of family is connection that results in multiplication. I think it's a shallow view to believe that God made Adam and Eve so they could enjoy sex and connection in an intimate way without the idea that there is something much deeper than that. Simply put, God has always valued connection with us.

Scripture shows us that the Father valued connection before humans were created, when He created us, and even after we sinned. He values connection so much that He sent His Son to the slaughter to pay the penalty of man's sins so that we could be reconnected to Him. Is Calvary about authority as a priority? I believe that is putting the cart before the horse. The reason that we do not see many leaders in the Kingdom of God truly making disciples in the way in which we are commanded to do in Scripture is that we don't understand the heart of the Father in Genesis chapters 1 and 2.

The Father wanted to be connected to Adam and Eve and He wanted their connection to result in one thing—family. When you see what Jesus did when He began His ministry, it actually screams Genesis 1 and 2. Through discipleship, Jesus connected in a very family way with those around Him. We spend so much time looking at the fact that we have been given back the authority stolen from us that we leave out the main reason we were created, which is to be a family with the Father. The second word in the Lord's prayer is *Father*. In short, God is a Father who has always wanted a family.

> We leave out the main reason we were created, which is to be a family with the Father.

We have spent so much time focusing on theology and ideology that we have largely ignored the methodology of Jesus Christ. His methodology in the Gospels was the same methodology found in Genesis 1 and 2. Jesus was more interested in surrounding Himself with family than He was in starting His own power healing and miracle ministry. We tend to focus on the twelve disciples He commanded to do power ministry to conquer the devil. However, this is not the full picture. If we are not careful, we will ignore the commandment that Jesus Christ gave in Matthew 28:19.

There is one word that will describe this end-time move, and that one word is *multiplication*. In the beginning, God commanded Adam and Eve to multiply, and He did that again through Jesus who gathered His own disciples. The methodology of God is family. Right now, the Father is dismantling religious structures in His church that do not reflect His passion for us to multiply. This end-time move of God before the return of His Firstborn will look like what it looked like before we turned our God-given authority over to satan.

There is evidence in the early church that the Greek idea of *oikos* is the method that overtook Rome. Rome was not declared a Christian nation because of power ministry, mass gatherings, books being written, or any of the other ways we think our current-day move of God is multiplying. The early church grew through family. *Oikos* was an extended family, united by a shared passion for following Jesus Christ, which became thicker than blood. These "family" communities multiplied literally all over the world.

Rodney Stark, in his book *The Rise of Christianity: How the Obscure, Marginal Jesus Movement Became the Dominant Religious Force in the Western World in a Few Centuries*, lays out a provocative thesis that essentially says that Christians valued family to such an extent that they thrived and multiplied until they actually out populated their pagan neighbors who held family in low regard. There is much that could be unpacked from Stark's ideas in this book, but the focus here is that the early church valued the concept of family, not just immediate blood relatives. And they valued the larger *oikos* or extended family united around a shared passion for following Jesus. The pagan culture around them saw the security and peace of their fellow Christians that flowed in part from the family and sense of community they shared, and they, the pagans, wanted some of it.

> **Family is and always will be messy, yet family is the cry of God's heart because He is a Father.**

God has a way of getting done what He sets out to do, and history tends to repeat itself. This reformation of the church that is at hand will be marked by the same DNA as that of Genesis chapters 1 and 2 and the ministry of Jesus as found in the Gospels. As the church stands on the cusp of this "old becoming new," we will see God crumble religious systems in His church so that they do not look new at all. This will be very difficult for many leaders in both the church and the marketplace who are used to a more Roman way of leading than a Genesis 1 and 2/Gospel way of leading. Life-on-life *oikos* is messy, and the church historically does not like messy. It prefers a system of control to keep things nice and tidy. Family is and always will be messy, yet family is the cry of God's heart because He is a Father.

Chapter 9

REFORMATION

highly doubt, when Paul wrote letters to those churches that we find in the New Testament, that he knew his words would be so influential in the message of Jesus Christ and His Father's kingdom. It is probably safe to say that Paul had no idea that what he wrote would one day end up in canonized Scripture, and 1,400 years later the printing press would take his words to every corner of the world. Did Luther realize the implications when he nailed his famous 95 Theses to that church door in Wittenberg, Germany on October 31, 1517? I don't think he or any of the Protestant Reformers quite knew the gravity of the situation. They were simply doing the best they could to follow what they believed God wanted them to do. It was an oppressive religious world back in that day. If you look closely at what is happening today you will begin to discern that perhaps another literal reformation is on deck right now, and few in the church quite know the gravity of the situation.

When Jesus ascended, we saw a beautiful thing happen in the church. Spiritual families began to form and multiply, and what ensued was a wildfire that could not be put out. There were outposts such as Antioch like we see in Acts 13 where apostles and prophets were leading and helping establish faith communities for the purpose of not only gathering but scattering as well. Over the next 300 years, the church was a beautiful expression of what the Father wanted in Genesis 1 and 2. Spiritual fathers and mothers were multiplying themselves all over the world through a family model of discipleship. If you take a look at the Bible and early church history, you will find that there is zero biblical precedent for the way in which we do church today. That may sound like an extreme statement to many, but give me some time to explain.

First, let me say this again plainly: *There is zero, and I mean zero biblical precedent for the way in which most churches in the world operate today.* In the early church, times of communion lasted for hours and were called love feasts. People gathered in someone's home and there would be a song, a word of encouragement given, a prayer for the sick or needy, laughter, and simply time for connection. The Holy Spirit was the undisputed leader in the room, and although there was an authority structure, it's not like what most people are used to today. It was warm, connecting, and everyone got the opportunity to play a part in whatever God was doing, not only in times of public gathering, but throughout the week as well.

This early church movement grew so abundantly that Rome took notice. Constantine knew that he had to do something because Christianity was not just an afterthought anymore. That fact that Rome was seen as a Christian nation around 300 years after the resurrection of Jesus Christ is mind-boggling. I used to think that was a great thing until I continued to study church history and the implications of this. Over time, what began to happen morphed into an absolute travesty for the church that Jesus laid His life down for. Men of power and control took the reins, and over the next thousand years or so the church drifted so far from its original design that it is actually scary to think about.

I personally used to wonder why so many professing Catholics have an affinity for the mother of our Lord. If I'm being honest, I have judged them for that, and I am sincerely sorry for ever doing so. A few years ago, the Father began to show me the "why" of this. What was obvious in the writings of Paul about Jesus introducing us to his Abba Father was not so obvious as time elapsed from the Ascension. Remember that the printing press was not available until the fifteenth century, meaning that Paul's letters to the church would not be distributed all over the world until long after they were written. There was a thousand-year gap in which satan had a heyday in misrepresenting the Father to millions and millions of people.

> The image of a tender Jesus who forgives and provides us a bridge to His loving Father was replaced with the image of a distant God who is not a Father at all and is constantly disappointed in people.

The church went under Roman influence in the early stages of its development. The Catholic system of religion became the theology, ideology, and methodology of the church for the most part. House churches were replaced with programs, and spiritual fathers and mothers were replaced with "authority figures," i.e. clergy who started to serve as the leaders of the church. The image of a tender Jesus who forgives and provides us a bridge to His loving Father was replaced with the image of a distant God who is not a Father at all and is constantly disappointed in people. No wonder so many Catholics were drawn to the more tender concept of Mary.

God was depicted as an angry task master. The concepts of family and community were replaced with organized religion that was about control, power, and eventually money. *Oikos* leaders were replaced by leaders who would turn into priests, cardinals, and eventually the ultimate leader who is the Pope. The message of grace exited stage left, replaced by a works-based mentality that would literally end up with people believing that they had to pay money to priests when their relatives died in order for the dead to be at peace with God.

Oh, how far the church drifted from Genesis 1 and 2. God always wanted a family that multiplied. When Jesus came to model the reality of our reconnection with God and how we could step back into the family the Father so desires, we started off well and then, within 300 years, it all collapsed. Satan realized that he could not defeat the church so he just joined the movement. The reality of a spiritual family that multiplied was replaced with a system of control and power that slowly drifted far away from the Father's original intention.

A Revelation of God's Grace

To say that God was approachable in the Old Testament could be considered a bit of a stretch. It seemed that the further man drifted from the Garden, the less approachable

God became. I sometimes preach on the passage in Leviticus 10 where God kills Aaron the high priest's sons Nadab and Abihu when they attempt to worship God without being asked to. God even told Moses one time that the people had better consecrate themselves because if they didn't, He was going to kill them and their animals. This is not an image of God that inspires us to want to cuddle up to Him. Yet, as we all know, things came into great focus at Calvary.

When we realize that not only was God's wrath satisfied by the atoning blood of His Son Jesus Christ, but also His kindness was poured out as well, it changes the way we understand God the Father. Yet even with this revelation that we now have, we must remember that this was not the case for most people when they thought about God from about 300 AD till the 15th century. The image that most people had of God was that He was unapproachable. There was no revelation of God's grace.

> The image that most people had of God was that He was unapproachable. There was no revelation of God's grace.

Years ago, I stumbled upon the story of a man named John Huss. For the longest time, I had credited Martin Luther and the other Reformers for helping change the world through the message of grace, but after reading up on Huss I see that Huss, who was strongly influenced by John Wycliffe, also played a significant role in the process. My purpose here is not to take a scholarly look at Huss. Instead, I want to briefly discuss what God used Huss (and then eventually Luther and others) to do so that we can see how God is currently setting the table for the current reformation.

Back when Huss came on the scene, most people viewed God as very distant. There was no revelation of grace. It is interesting to note that although Gutenberg designed the European version of moveable type to create his printing press and, in 1455 printed, in Latin, one of the most stunningly beautiful copies of the Bible known as the *Biblia Sacra*, it wasn't until 1535 that the world would have the first complete Bible in the English language. Even at that, there was a rocky path to be trod before printed copies of the Bible became available to the general public. One of the biggest roadblocks was the church's effort to prevent the Bible from being translated from Latin to English and made available to the laity. Eventually, that effort was thwarted and the Word of God became available to everyone, but not without struggle. The devil fought hard to keep people from knowing that God wants to be our Father and that, because of Jesus, we have an invitation to be close friends with the Most High God by walking in intimacy and obedience with Him.

Stumbling Upon the Gospel

If you study history, you can see how the hand of God lead various Reformers, hundreds of years apart, to stumble upon what would eventually change the world yet again— the Gospel. Huss was influenced by the writings of John

Wycliffe, and eventually Huss' writings would influence the Reformers who followed him. One hundred years later they would find their way into the hands of Martin Luther, whose work would profoundly change the church and the world.

Huss' teachings on grace became so popular that he was surrounded by followers who were called Hussites. His message on the love of God and salvation in Jesus Christ opposed the religious structure of control that dominated the landscape of Huss' day. As he became more and more popular, the religious establishment of power ended up killing him to stop his message from growing. Within 100 years, Luther and other Reformers started challenging popular theology, and for the first time since the early church the message of God as a Father of love began to reemerge. When the message of grace appeared on the scene, the Protestant Reformation started to unfold. So, in short, the Reformation was specifically about theology.

My professor of theology at Beeson Divinity School has the greatest definition of theology I've ever heard. Dr. Fisher Humphreys told me 25 years ago in school that theology is simply "thinking about God." Most people don't consider themselves theologians, but in fact we all are to some extent. God has placed eternity in the hearts of every person ever born, and at some point each one of us will at the very least ponder theological questions such as where we are from, where we are going, why we are on the earth, and who God is. And most of us will develop some sort of theology to answer those questions.

In Huss' day, the church's theology of God was not in line with the revelation of Jesus Christ. Instead, there was a "works-based" theology that had people trying to satisfy God. When you look deeply into the Scriptures you find that God has not changed. At the core of Himself, God has always valued connection with others. He did not become loving and tender at the cross. Rather, when we dig into Scripture we see that He has always desired to be in close proximity and relationship to us. So what Huss and Luther and others stumbled upon that led to the Reformation has been imbedded in Scripture all along. Not only did Romans and Galatians help the Reformers better understand the true nature of God, but going back into the Old Testament we see what God was really like all along. Yes, He had a severe aspect, but He has always also been a loving and tender God who desires to be in relationship with us.

> **At the core of Himself, God has always valued connection with others. He did not become loving and tender at the cross.**

Genesis 1:26 says, "Let *us* make man in our image." While we know that "us" means the Triune God, if you are courageous enough to read the Bible for yourself, and I mean *really read it*, you will find that not only was the Triune God a reality before the earth was made, but there was also a council-community-family around God as well. There are many Scriptures in both the Old Testament and New Testament that point to this. Verse 1 in Psalm 82 says, *"God has taken his place in the divine council; in the midst of the gods he holds judgment"* (ESV). We also know from Scripture that a rebellion took place in Heaven, and as a result of this rebellion God cast many who were part of this council out of His domain. The Bible says He cast one third of these celestial beings out of the domain of Heaven (see Rev. 12:4). Further reading of Scripture indicates that this rebellion and casting out took place in the beginning (see 1 John 3:8-12). So it follows that the serpent in the Garden was a fallen celestial being (or perhaps satan himself—there is theological divergence on this point).

The true nature of God—His tender, loving nature—was on display before humans were created. God had a council in the Heavenlies and a family in Genesis 1 and 2. But because of the work of one of His fallen beings, there was a disconnection in Heaven and then another disconnection in the Garden. Yet God is never taken by surprise. Jesus existed with God before the foundation of the world to fulfill God's plan of redemption so that we could be reunited with our loving Heavenly Father. God planned the sacrifice of His own blood before the foundation of the earth in order to get His family of humans back before humans even sinned! What does this tell us about God? It tells us lots of things, among them that God has always valued family, and He has always been a loving Father.

Methodological Reformation

The first Reformation was theological. Many signs are pointing to this new reformation of the church as being not only theological but also methodological. This current reformation is about the Father getting His family back. In this end-time move of God, He is coming to reveal Himself as the Father who values family. The model of God's family will look dramatically different than the model of what the church has looked like for the last 1,700 years. God is raising up leaders in His own kingdom who are spiritual fathers and mothers who will lead faith communities that look way more like the early church than the church has since 300 AD. God is dismantling the theology, ideology, and methodology of the current church so that He can usher in His new/old paradigm of church and its methodology.

Years ago I cried out to God and told Him that I honestly just wanted to know Him. I didn't care what He did with me, how He used me, or what I would accomplish with my life. I simply wanted to know Him. I remember praying, "Father, I want to be so close to You that I don't even know where I begin and You end. I want to be intertwined with You in literal covenant. I want to be friends with You." My prayers stood on the promise of two passages—Jeremiah 9:23-24 and Philippians 3:7-10. Jeremiah spoke of knowing God intimately, and Paul did the same at the end of his life.

What does it look like to know God intimately? Just look at Jesus in the Gospels and you will see. Jesus spent all night praying to His Father before He picked those He would disciple and who would become His "family" in that season. He was constantly going to the Father in prayer. Father, Son, and Holy Spirit were and are "family." We know from Scripture that even at the young age of twelve, Jesus was strong in His theology. By the time He was thirty years old, He was demonstrating both strong theology and strong methodology in the ways He went about His ministry leading up to the cross.

> ## What does it look like to know God intimately? Just look at Jesus in the Gospels and you will see.

I believe that this new reformation will look like the life of Jesus. Just as Luther and the Reformers gave the world a new theology, this new reformation will continue to tell us what God is like while also showing us the "what and the where" of the ideology and methodology of His kingdom.

The ways in which the church operates are forever changing until the return of the Lord Jesus Christ. Right now God is dismantling the structure of the church as we know it and taking it back to its roots so that the new structure He is putting in place will look strikingly similar to what the church looked like for the first 300 years after the ascension of Jesus. Small is the new big. The death of the celebrity spirit is at hand.

The Father, who has always valued family, wants His family back. The new model of church will look like a family on a mission together through the lens of gathering in His presence, gathering in homes, and scattering into the city. It will look like leaders developing cultures of habitation that form a literal biblical model of discipleship-multiplication that sows itself into cities. This is the model of biblical

Christianity, and I believe we will begin to see all other models of church submit to this model.

Houses of prayer will replace fancy programs. Great speakers and talented musicians who lead the masses to sit in seats only to return and do the same thing week after week will give way to spiritual fathers and mothers who open their homes as embassies of discipleship while being submitted to true spiritual authority. When this happens, the church will grow in the West like it has been growing in China and Iran through the model of Matthew 28:19, because the template of this new reformation has its roots in Scripture itself.

Jesus came not only to show us who the Father is, but He also came to model what our lives are supposed to look like. Millions of people have loved God over the years, but not nearly as many people have been interested in orbiting their lives around the same patterns that we find in the Scriptures. Theology is important but so is ideology and methodology, so much so that it will be the backbone of this end-time move of God. Before the Lord Jesus Christ returns, the church is going back to its roots. Success counted by the number of people showing up for a gathering will be replaced by success counted by the number of disciples multiplied through the vehicle of spiritual family.

Heaven's score card looks different than what we have thought for far too long. God loves us, and we should be so thankful for what the Protestant Reformation brought to the church, but there is currently a massive missing ingredient, and that is the ingredient of discipleship through the lens of family that multiplies. The "what and how" of the kingdom is the focus at hand. When we can grasp how the church overtook Rome before Constantine took control of it, we will find that the current reformation is actually an old recipe. We (the church) are going "back to the start." As we discover the "how" of the movement that overtook Rome, we will be inspired to orbit our lives around this same "how," this same methodology. The new reformation is about Matthew 28. How thankful we all should be for what happened in that first Reformation when Luther and the others began to unfold the reality of God's grace and kindness to us. All of these years later, we are now here with that same intensity toward the model that the same God of the Reformation prefers. That model is family, a family that multiplies.

Chapter 10

MULTIPLICATION

Not too long ago I was in Gig Harbor, Washington and a seasoned prophetess gave my wife and me some words of knowledge and prophecy that helped me discern how God has wired me. This sister in Christ gave quite a few accurate words from the Lord over Wendy and me, but one stood out the most. It was actually the first word that she spoke over me. She said, "The Lord shows me that you have always been curious, and you are His inquisitive one." This stuck out to me because ever since I was a little boy, I have found myself being constantly curious about God and His kingdom. Even before I made a declaration of my faith in Jesus Christ publicly, I tended to think about God, His ways, the afterlife, why I'm here, and what really matters in life.

Questions have always driven me. While many people ask questions from a posture of cynicism, I can honestly say that my questions have always been from a place of genuine curiosity. When I was 12 years old, I asked my parents why disciples of Jesus Christ don't raise the dead and open blind eyes like the disciples in the Bible did. Little did I know that one day God would use me to do some very unusual things like that.

A Culture of Discipleship

I have lost count of the questions I have asked the Father all of these years, but I will never forget where I was when He asked me a question that I did not know the answer to. I have learned over the years that when God asks me a question, it's not because He does not know the answer, but because I don't. I was at the beach and God asked me, "How will you lead the church I am calling you to lead?" I had just taken the job as lead pastor of a church, and although I had a passion for God and some experience with preaching, I knew that this was a loaded question. I responded with a question back to Jesus, and His answer is literally still driving me to this day. I said, "Lord, if You were here leading this church, what would You do?" He said, "I would make disciples."

A culture of discipleship requires a leader to choose the path of humility because the backbone of the method in which Jesus did His ministry was all about relinquishment. Think about this for a moment: If Jesus wanted to, He could have created an attractional model around His divinity, gifts, influence, and popularity with the masses. What is an attractional model? Let's look at the normal experience for a person who has given his or her life to Jesus Christ and attends a church. Show up on a Sunday morning and sing a little bit together with some other saints and then listen to the same preacher over and over each Sunday; tithe; serve occasionally, usually through a teaching platform, student ministry volunteer position, or as a greeter; and listen to popular teachers at other churches through podcasts or other media platforms.

> A culture of discipleship requires a leader to choose the path of humility.

Obviously, this is an overgeneralization, but you get my point. For most of the churches in the literal world, you will find that they are built upon the premise of the attractional idea. The church has become so filled with consumerism that you will hear things like this on a weekly basis: "I'm not being fed here anymore. This church does not fit what I need. I don't like this style of worship..." and so on.

Can you imagine how many people would have gathered for weekly services if Jesus had led the way most pastors and leaders in both the church and marketplace do leadership today? Half the world would have come to be a part of His services. So why then did Jesus run from the masses and spend most of His time in small *oikos* raising up other leaders? Well, to understand this, we must go all the way back to Genesis 1 and 2. The first thing that Jesus did when He began His ministry was to surround Himself with those people of peace whom the Father had ordained for Him to mentor. As far as I can tell as I study the Scriptures for myself, Jesus modeled to us that He spent most of His time mentoring a small group of people who would eventually, even in their own brokenness, change the world. How astounding that we get to watch the Father in the Gospels through Jesus. So why don't we, as followers of Jesus who have been given an assignment from the Lord, do the same?

There has been much time spent, and rightfully so, studying the theology we find in the Gospels, but what is exploding all over the world right now in unassuming places is the model of Jesus that we see in the Gospels themselves. Jesus did what the Father did in the Garden. He was with a family as their leader and provider and His expectation was that they would go and multiply. I am not exaggerating when I say that it is almost impossible to find a ministry that is truly built upon the premise of multiplication. Almost all ministries and mindsets in the church today are built upon the premise of addition and attraction. The way in which I often teach on this is with a picture of an oil funnel. If you turn an oil funnel with the wide end up, you will find this to be a picture of how most leaders in the church operate. We recruit as many people as possible to follow our vision with marketing, social media recruiting, and advertising in an effort to capture "customers" to stay around as long as possible. However, if you turn the oil funnel upside down, you see more of a picture of what Jesus did.

Let's revisit for a moment how Jesus grew His church. He spent much of His time specifically mentoring three men out of His twelve disciples. Those three men, and the other disciples, relying on Jesus' model of discipleship, went into all the known world with the Gospel. Some 300 years later the church Jesus started had taken off to such an extent that Rome took notice. As a matter of fact, when Jesus died, His church exploded. Contrast that with the church today. When a leader dies today, their ministry typically crumbles. Why?

The answer is not as complicated as it seems. There are two things in play as to why ministries and companies crumble when the leader leaves. A lack of humility and lack of a culture of multiplication have taken down many organizations. Maybe, just maybe, things are changing. If we look closely enough, we will discover that there is a biblical methodology that can change the current church paradigm.

> **When Jesus died, His church exploded. Contrast that with the church today. When a leader dies today, their ministry typically crumbles.**

What I began to do ten years ago is to question, and I mean really question, the model of the church not only in the West but in the world. During that time, God opened doors for me to travel and minister in various churches even outside of America. What I noticed was that every single church I ministered in was operating in an attractional model. Why does the model of most ministries, and dare I even say marketplace areas, look like an attractional model when the Lord we say we love so much modeled a completely opposite way of doing things while He was here? Jesus didn't have a worship leader or a building He reported to where He preached every week. In fact, most scholars agree that Jesus only did public ministry for 18 of the 36 months of His 3 year ministry.

Today the church has thousands upon thousands of teachings on how Jesus came to reveal the Father, and how kind the Father is, and how much He loves people, but what about teachings that examine *how* He did these things? Why aren't we teaching on the methods Jesus used? I think this is a very relevant question for both the ministry world and the marketplace. Churches and companies that set the structure of their spheres of influence upon the basis of multiplication automatically attract Heaven's favor. Why? Because this is the heart of the Father. It has always been the heart of the Father. God is a God of multiplication.

The celebrity spirit so prevalent in both the church and marketplace today disdains the discipleship model because it takes the focus off of the leader and places it in the hands of those who are being discipled. I believe we are seeing God eradicate this celebrity spirit from His ecclesia by the teachings that are rising up against it (read the book of Jude) and also by the demolition of the structures themselves. Nothing, and I mean *nothing*, will remove the celebrity spirit from an organization like establishing a true biblical model of *oikos* (spiritual family that multiplies). God is raising up cultures of discipleship all over the world, and many years from now church historians will look back and say about this time that this was the methodological reformation that swept through both the church and marketplace structures.

I have been greatly influenced by Jim Collins and his books, particularly *Good to Great*, in which he discusses the differences between good leaders and great leaders. Jim points out that great leaders are not only humble, but they also have succession plans. According to Collins, great leaders always plan to work themselves out of a job. While celebrity spirit pastors are prideful and territorial, great leaders are the opposite. When you read the Gospels you see that Jesus was the exact opposite of prideful and territorial. In John 14:12 He says, "*I tell you the truth, anyone who believes in me will do the same works I have done, and even greater works, because I am going to be with the Father*" (NLT). Greater things? It is hard to imagine any one of us doing greater things than Jesus, yet He says that we will. This from the Son of God, God in the flesh, who takes out a towel in the upper room and washes the feet of those He knew would betray Him. The path of Philippians 2 is mind-boggling when you realize that Jesus lowered Himself to the lowest place, even to the point of death, and it was then that the Father elevated Him to the highest place.

> **We are churning out church leaders who have little or no understanding of the true biblical model of church.**

How did I go to a distinguished seminary that was rigorous and yet never have one single conversation about how to make disciples? If Jesus was so clear about multiplication in His command to His disciples, why then are most ministries in the world about addition and not multiplication? Why are seminaries not teaching discipleship/multiplication? We are churning out church leaders who have little or no understanding of the true biblical model of church. Will we begin to see this new reformation hit our seminaries and Bible colleges? I believe so, but not without resistance.

The Gumbo Principle

In the final three chapters of this book, I am going to walk you through three steps that I call *Tent, Home,* and *City.* Over the past ten years, God has been showing me that these are the steps necessary to the development of a culture of multiplication for both ministries and the marketplace. While these steps are simple to understand, they have proven, in my experience, to be very difficult to implement. These three steps are the key to attracting the favor of the Father upon your life and what you are called to lead, but be warned—as you walk these out you are likely to experience warfare. There will be ground fire and air attacks from the enemy who wants you to just stick with the attractional model. Reformers always experience resistance, but with God on your side, you can walk this out. How? Well, I walk it out in part with what I call "the gumbo principle."

As you now know, food is a favorite pastime of mine. And although I have surrendered food to God, I still enjoy good food and I enjoy cooking it. About ten years ago, I stumbled upon a recipe for New Orleans gumbo that would prove to be simple to understand but difficult to pull off. Cooking is one of my favorite hobbies, especially when I just want to unplug and relax. I enjoy finding different recipes and trying them out. When I stumbled upon the gumbo recipe, I definitely wanted to try it. The whole thing looked pretty simple on paper. The recipe calls for flour, canola oil, celery, onion, green pepper, chicken stock, chicken, sausage, shrimp, and spices. Jumping in eagerly with both feet, my first attempt at this recipe proved to be seriously challenging because of the roux. What is a roux, you ask? It's a mixture of oil and flour used to make sauces. Simple, right? It's simple once you learn the correct ratio of oil and flour, and then patiently stir for the right amount of time (between 70 to 90 minutes depending upon the color of the roux) over the proper temperature. You even have to develop the proper pace at which to stir.

I have learned the secrets to perfect roux—the perfect skillet, temperature, spoon, and pace of the stirring. I am proud to say that my roux is so good it has spoiled me to where I can't eat anyone else's gumbo. My gumbo is slow and boring to make, and it can drive me crazy sometimes. If you don't know how to make a proper roux and don't know the timing of adding the veggies, you may have gumbo, but it will be very average. All this to say that what can look simple can actually be quite hard to do.

> **What can look simple can actually be quite hard to do.**

Walking out the three steps of *Tent, Home,* and *City* is a bit like making good New Orleans gumbo. These three steps may appear simple on the surface but will prove much more difficult to implement because they are time-consuming and contradict what most of us have been told is proper methodology. Yet if you're willing, these steps will walk you through a biblical model of leadership that can shift your church, your business, and even your family. They are a prototype of this current reformation.

Life is short for each of us. God desires that we live strong as we wrestle with those things that come against our walk of faith. Dig in with me on these final three chapters as I dare you to implement these three steps into what God is doing in your life.

Chapter 11

Tent: Gathering around His Presence

Great stories are typically those that come with twists and turns. I want to tell the story of how a literal 20k-dollar tent, donated by some very generous businessmen, ended up on our property here at Bridgeway Church. This tent is where we now gather to pray. But let me back up a bit and talk about how the Father led me to even consider this.

Around the year 2003, some friends of mine started a prayer group at the church I was attending. This was my introduction to corporate intercession. Obviously, I had prayed off and on and read some of the classics by E.M. Bounds, Andrew Murray, and other writers who focused heavily on prayer. But honestly, I had not been part of any type of intercessory group. The idea of sitting in a room and praying for more than twenty minutes or so honestly made me anxious. I was not wired to do something like that at the time. I would occasionally visit those times of intercessory prayer at our church, but my visits were sporadic at best. I was more interested in praying for the sick. I love praying for people with physical needs. God has used me to help many others learn how to be part of healing ministry, but as for intercession, I left that to those who were called to that sort of thing. I laugh a little bit now because I am one of "those people," but back then I really shied away from intercession. It simply was not a practice of mine to spend extended times of prayer with other people. I'm sure some of you can relate, which is one reason I think we don't see more houses of prayer.

All of that changed when I met a man named Michael Thornton, who I have already mentioned is the author of

Fire in the Carolinas. When I met Michael, a relationship was formed. In our conversations over the next few years, something began to come into focus for me. The term *David's Tabernacle* came up often as Michael talked about what King David did when he took leadership in Jerusalem. Although I have taught many times about the story of David and Saul and what happened in First and Second Samuel, it never, ever dawned on me how David set up his rulership when he was fully established in Jerusalem. Sometimes I wonder if God conceals things because He is having fun on His end, and when it's time for things not to be concealed anymore He opens our eyes to what we are supposed to see. It was either that or complete ignorance on my part, but when I realized there is actually a formula imbedded into the method of King David's leadership that is found in Scripture, my wheels started turning.

I began to ask the Father and the leadership team at Bridgeway Church why we were not establishing a culture of prayer at Bridgeway. God took me back to the story of Jim Cymbala and how Jim simply started praying at Brooklyn Tabernacle, the church that he was called to lead. When Jim and his wife Carol began to pray, things changed at that church. His book *Fresh Fire* stirred my soul in seminary. When I began to dig into the story of David in the Scriptures, I was struck by the revelation of his method. Simply put, David was a king, but he actually began his kingship looking more like a priest. David actually paid people a great deal of money to pray and worship Yahweh.

The more I studied David's method, the more God began to connect the dots for me—David's favor in Jerusalem came about as a result of the relationship he built with God in the secret place. When his kingship manifested, the anointing that was on him was not the only thing that gave David success. It was also the culture of prayer and worship he created that made a place for God to inhabit that brought success. David's anointing led him to implement a method that would be the recipe for God to move in Jerusalem in unprecedented ways. In fact, the longest reign of peace and prosperity in Israel was when David sat on the throne.

> **David was a king, but he actually began his kingship looking more like a priest.**

If you know anything about the role of a king in the Old Testament, it was unheard of for a king to wear an ephod and play the part of a priest, yet King David did just that. David was concerned with one thing in His life more than anything, and that was to create a habitation for the presence of God. He was a man after God's own heart. In the Scriptures we see his progression through Bethlehem, Hebron, and on to Jerusalem as the progression through one single glaring core value in his life—to host God's presence through intimacy, prayer, and worship. It was unheard of to spend as much money as David spent on prayer and worship, yet he did because he had his priorities set on God the Father.

If you read the early sections of the book of Revelation, you will find that even right now at this very moment, Heaven has literal elders who exist to worship the Lord God Almighty at all times. Where are the churches with elders whose job description is simply to be the lead priest who focuses on God's presence around the clock? We have replaced His presence with programs. God wants His family back to gather around His presence. If intercession is as unappealing to you as it was to me, ask for the spirit of wisdom and revelation (see Eph. 1:17) and begin to beseech God to give you a passion for what Heaven is passionate about. When you put up a prayer *Tent* (whether literal or simply a designated room) and make it the focus of everything you do, you will find out very quickly how the *Tent* both stirs up warfare around you while also attracting uncommon favor on what you are doing.

Creating a Culture of Habitation for God

As you begin to establish a culture of prayer in your sphere of influence, you can rest assured that you will go through some interference from the enemy. It's simply a part of the process and it's always worth it.

James says that if we draw near to God, then He will draw near to us (see James 4:8). God is indeed enthroned on the praises of His people.

A friend and mentor of mine, Gary Hippolyte, runs the House of Prayer in Croix-des-Bouquets, Haiti. When he and his wife, Linda, started their prayer ministry in that area of

Haiti, anything that could go wrong went wrong for two or three years. The Father did not tell Gary that Croix-des-Bouquets had more voodoo temples than anywhere else in Haiti. Gary and Linda faced so much warfare in Haiti in those early years that it seemed like they had made a mistake by even going there. Yet they persisted, and the stories from those early years read like something out of the book of Acts. My point is this—as you embark upon creating a culture of prayer and worship in your church or business, you will likely become very familiar with Ephesians 6:12: *"For our struggle is not against flesh and blood, but against the rulers, against the authorities, against the powers of this dark world and against the spiritual forces of evil in the Heavenly realms."*

> **There is nothing that the devil hates more than a family, church, or business establishing a true culture of prayer and worship.**

There is nothing that the devil hates more than a family, church, or business establishing a true culture of prayer and worship that has zero celebrity spirit attached to it, where the Holy Spirit is the leader and the assignment is to simply minister unto the Lord. For a church or business in the West, this whole idea seems ridiculous because, for many people, they simply don't understand the point. I have lost count of how many times I have either led events or attended events that have been well attended because they were centered around healing or deliverance. We hosted such an event at

Bridgeway a few years ago and there were over 1,500 people in attendance. But when I call prayer meetings, a fraction of that many people show up. Yet it is at these prayer meetings that the literal glory of God manifests unlike in other gatherings.

One of the passions of my life is mentoring business leaders. I love nothing more than seeing the Father use marketplace leaders to extend His kingdom. Over the years I have seen two key principals help leaders in the marketplace to see God touch what they are building. These two principals are: 1) resign any and all ownership of the business to God—literally name Him CEO and put that in a document, and 2) establish a culture of prayer in the business. This sounds quite simple, yet it is ignored by many business leaders—leaders who do in fact love God very much. Until a marketplace leader places God as the literal leader of the business and develops a culture of prayer in that business, he or she can actually be hindering God from moving and not even know it.

Did David have so much success because he was anointed? I don't think so. David gave everything over to God and established a literal culture of prayer and worship in Israel. If you look objectively at both the marketplace and church in today's culture, you will have a hard time finding many places that do that. The Father is looking for leaders who will do what King David did in terms of establishing a true culture of God-focused prayer and worship. When this happens in organizations, things change for the better and

God begins to do things in those companies and churches that other organizations don't see happening.

Instead of leading whatever God has called you to lead through your anointing or intellectual capital, go ahead and create an ecosystem driven by His presence. Jump into the biblical narrative of David and see how he did it in his tenure over Israel. Ask yourself why Jesus spent so much time in prayer. Perhaps in a world where so many people find little purpose, this can be the first step in discovering one of the reasons we are here in the first place. I have personally seen students at our Ascent University come alive as they come into the culture of prayer at Bridgeway.

We have come a long way at Bridgeway, and there are no plans to go back. Programs have been replaced with presence-driven times of prayer and worship, and the fruit of this in our local community here is undeniable. God is leading His ministers to enter the land of Zadok where the ultimate desire is for churches, companies, and families to simply minister unto the Lord. There is a purification that God is doing in His ecclesia. The first step in this model of reformation is to place His presence as the first priority, not just in private times of prayer but also in public time of connection to the Father, such as corporate intercession.

A Christian leader does not need God to draw people around a vision in order to be successful. If someone has enough money, they can create programs, marketing, and other focused initiatives that capture people's attention so that they will be drawn to participate on some level. That's cultural Christianity, and it is perhaps the curse of the day. God is raising up leaders who care more about His presence than their own platforms and agendas. God is raising up leaders who are transforming the culture of their organizations so that He is the famous one. He is redirecting His church in such a way that it will feel like a deconstruction. The Father is dismantling structures that do not place the priority of His presence at the forefront.

> **A Christian leader does not need God to draw people around a vision in order to be successful.**

In America, one of the things that I have noticed over the years is how many churches orbit around the teaching gift of one person. This method is dangerous because it slowly places that teacher's gift as the rallying point of the flock. It is the perfect recipe for the celebrity spirit to manifest. God is raising up leaders who simply want to minister to Him without the platforms of huge ministries or notoriety. I believe we will begin to see businesses open up a room in their buildings as a place for employees to literally pray and worship. CEOs will begin to take a posture of humility and resign from their jobs and invite God to be the CEO. Houses of prayer will literally transform businesses and bring a level of favor in the marketplace that connecting cannot.

If you truly want to see God do unexplainable things in your organization, whether it be a church or business, start literally gathering around His presence and give the entire organization to Him. Colossians 3:23 says that we are to do everything "unto the Lord" and not for man. A leader who desires to worship God simply because He is worthy to be worshiped is placing him or herself into the position to be rightly aligned with Heaven's preferred template. Twenty-four/seven worship is actually going on right now around the throne of God. Why wait when you can be a part of the Father's methodology here and now?

A temptation for many leaders who actually desire to turn their organization into a house of prayer will be for them to seek to emulate another organization that is already doing that. For me, it's refreshing to know that what the Father wants to do all over the world with different leaders is help them be "them" as they develop cultures of prayer. In other words, don't feel the pressure to be like someone else. Let the Father define what your own culture of prayer will look and feel like.

Chapter 12

HOME: CREATING DISCIPLESHIP COMMUNITY

Recently I sat down in my room and played the soundtrack of the Pixar movie *Up* and cried like a baby. Just me and Jesus and a bunch of tears. It seems like yesterday when I took my then five-year-old to see *Up*. I have never been more ambushed in my life by a plot. I was traveling and speaking to some teenagers near Birmingham, Alabama and had some time to take my son Sam to see this movie. Thirty minutes into it, I was squalling.

Up is the story of a man who loved his wife and then lost her to death. Her death sets the scene for a really funny journey that this man goes on with a lonely little boy. Both the older man and the young boy are longing for a place in their hearts called "home," although it takes them some time and many adventures together to realize this. Actually, the boy realizes it way before the older man does, but isn't that just like the wisdom of a child. Anyway, the first 30 minutes of the movie rip at your emotions because you realize just how fast life can go by.

Our son Sam is going off to college soon, and I'm starting to feel some of the feelings portrayed in the movie. "How did things go by so fast? Why can't we slow life down? Why does it hurt so bad to lose what we once had?" I am happy for Sam, and I realize that his two siblings are up next, and before I know it Wendy and I will be empty nesters. We'll still have our nest, but it is going to look different. The sense of community we have enjoyed as a family is shifting. The life-on-life experiences Wendy and I have shared with our children are changing and will continue to change. The spiritual capital we poured into them is bearing fruit in our three amazing kids, and I'm so thankful to God. But the sense of family we have enjoyed for so long is shifting, and I am going to miss it.

Why is community so important to humans? Because God wired us that way. We are meant to do life with others. Jesus knew this and modeled His ministry around the concept of home/community through the rabbinic method of discipleship. When I talk about *Home* here, I am talking about a model where a spiritual mentor who has higher spiritual capital than his or her disciples is modeling a life-on-life experience where it is natural to bond with God deeply, and loving others well is the outflow of that bond. *Home* looks like going high up the mountain of God and then following Him as He shows you who to shoulder-tap and invite into a discipling relationship.

We are meant to do life with others.

While the nuclear family is wonderfully biblical and profitable, the idea of *Home* as discussed here is not relegated to natural families only. Whether it's a married couple discipling in their home or a single person leading in her home, the model includes someone who has high spiritual capital and a life worth imitating doing what Jesus did by following the Father's instructions to disciple others. Side note for the godly singles among us: Be of *great* cheer! Jesus was the *ultimate* disciple-maker and He did it without ever bearing the natural title of father or husband. It's not your experience in the natural that qualifies you. It's your maturity in the Spirit that does. Let's be honest with ourselves—there are simply not many people who really make disciples the way Jesus did. Why? Well, it's hard because it makes us vulnerable. And because, unfortunately, many leaders don't have a life worth imitating.

The Path of Humility

As I have wrestled with the changes in our family life, I find myself spending lots of time asking the Father about my purpose on earth. That may sound ridiculous considering I am almost fifty years old and the pastor of a church, but I am in a very reflective season and it's causing me to question things. The journey to a high level of friendship with God and influence for Him almost always goes through the path of humility. It's in these seasons where we find a deeper level of who God is and what we are actually made of.

> **God is destroying the celebrity spirit in the church and will raise up churches that show people how to make disciples who make disciples.**

I know many well-known ministers who have influential platforms. They love God with all their heart and give away intellectual capital and even use their gifts to help people have an encounter with the Lord, but they themselves do not disciple others. There are wonderfully gifted leaders all over the Body of Christ who serve God in various ways, but they simply don't make disciples. The church in China and Iran is exploding right now because its leaders value godly multiplication.

Why don't more churches have a biblical model of discipleship? As I mentioned before, I think in part it is because many leaders don't have a life worth imitating. It's easier to hide behind a spiritual gift given from the Father to accomplish a task than it is to invite a disciple into your real life to see the good, bad, and ugly. Discipleship is messy, time consuming, hard, and often disappointing because real people with real problems take up our heart space and leave us hurting. And as imperfect disciple-makers, we're capable of doing the same. Discipleship is risky for everyone involved. Jesus never sinned against anyone He discipled, but His perfection didn't quarantine Him from risk. If there is anyone who understands being vulnerable and feeling rejection in return, it's Jesus. Vulnerable relationships are more complicated than simple and predictable church services. Walking out our own vulnerability can be seriously challenging, as I know personally, yet God will always be with us in the process.

Encountering God

I had two significant encounters with the Lord that really shaped me as a leader. The first came about as a result of a word from a seasoned intercessor in my life. The word was that God was going to give me a radical encounter, and this would happen according to God's timing, not mine. My thought was, "Well, God, if this is You, then that's fine with me."

When I look back on the last fifty years of my life and read the Scriptures for myself, I see a constant theme of unusual stories. The Bible is the most extraordinary book I've ever read, and in my leadership I simply don't want to be a part of a culture that is not open to the God of the Bible. What you read in Scripture isn't fantasy. It is full of real experiences that happened to real people. I promise you that Moses was not in the back of that desert looking for a burning bush. Yet God showed up through that bizarre encounter. If someone wrote about a similar experience today, there are plenty of people who would write it off as crazy. Many churches would never consider allowing the gifts of the Spirit to be in operation because that would threaten the financial structure of their churches. We are much more comfortable with "usual" than unusual.

Years ago, I preached a sermon on having faith to raise the dead. The pastor of a large local church called me and had many questions about the fact that I even preached such a sermon. I had just spent some time with Surprise Sithole in South Africa and my faith was stirred because at the time he had raised 10 people from the dead. My point is this—we are the ones who have limited God. If we will truly be open to Him being the Lord of our lives, perhaps we will see more stories in our own lives like those we read about in the Bible. God will do things "out of the box" because to Him they are not out of the box. God does not have a box. We are the ones who want to control Him and create our own image of what He is supposed to be like.

> God will do things "out of the box" because to Him they are not out of the box. God does not have a box.

I told God many years ago, "I'm sick of reading stories like Philip being translated to another place and doing incredible things for You when I don't see stuff like that in my life." That was twenty years ago and I'm not going to write all of the things down that I have seen with my own eyes, but I can promise you that faith is the currency of Heaven and God will meet you where your hunger is. I have journal entries from many years ago that said, "God, You showed Paul Heavenly things and I am Your son too. I want it all, God." He apparently remembers our prayers. When that seasoned intercessor gave me that word, I was ready, and not too long after I had an unusual encounter that to this day makes me scratch my head.

Trying to explain what it was like is very difficult. I was standing in the front of our sanctuary during a worship service when I was taken up and saw Heaven. I began to cry so hard that someone on our security team asked me if I was okay. I was crying so hard I could barely breathe as joy flooded my emotions. I saw a crystal river winding toward this city where a sound that I can't explain was thundering out of an area with an incredibly bright light. I saw thousands upon thousands of people waving banners and worshiping together. I saw the greenest grass I've ever seen. Some of the people were looking at me. The sound of Heaven was a symphony of praise and I was weeping tears of joy. It was an amazing foretaste of Heaven that can never be fully explained in words.

The other encounter that I want to share was the exact opposite in terms of emotions. It was so matter-of-fact that I kept thinking as it was happening, "This is so real. This is real." I don't know whether or not I was in my body. When I say, "I stood with a man," I mean just that. I felt myself being pulled up out of the earthly realm to where I was standing in front of a man dressed in white. His clothes were not like the clothes that most of us wear here on earth. He was wearing a very simple long white robe. He had a very long beard. I felt like I had known him my entire life. Then he spoke to me. "You are about to go through a hard season where the Father will train you," he said.

As I looked to my right, I saw these gigantic horses. When I say gigantic, they were at least five times the size of normal horses and they were stomping their hooves. The man did not tell me what the horses were there for, but I somehow knew that these were war horses that would battle against demonic forces that were going to try to stop what God was going to do through my life. If you had told me that I would write something like this in a book, I would not have believed it. Yet I fear God more than I fear man, so let me finish the story.

The man in white then looked at me and began to tell me about God's plans for me. He told me some things that I have pondered in my heart since that day. I looked right at him and said, "Why is God doing this?" The man said to me, "You value multiplication." I woke up out of this experience so dramatically that I was stunned. It was more real than anything I've ever experienced. It was not like some faint dream where you can't remember the details.

Currently, we have a culture of multiplication at Bridgeway and Ascent University, and a higher level of love and grit developing in us as we step into multiplication, so in hindsight this Heavenly encounter was very confirming for what God is doing here in the Bridgeway Church community.

Recipe for Reformation

I have noticed over the last ten years or so that you will have a hard time finding a leader in the church or marketplace who does not agree in theory with the need for God's presence (*Tent*) and for community (*Home*), but when you start to discuss what this actually looks like in practice, that is where the disagreements come into play. Anyone can go buy the ingredients to cook gumbo, but that is only where the fun begins. Until you learn how to stir that roux, you may have what looks like gumbo, but the real thing only comes from the correct way to make those ingredients come together.

When I say *Home*, I am not talking about connecting in community where you know people's names and you don't feel as alone as you used to. I am referring to the literal ideology and method that Jesus showed us around the reality of discipleship. This has been very humbling to Wendy and me over the years because developing a culture of discipleship is not easy. As a matter of fact, it is the single hardest thing I have ever put my hand to. We all need a good humbling along the way, and if you really want to be humbled, sincerely seek to establish a culture of discipleship where God has you planted. It is much easier and neater to have an ethos that is known for predictable programs. Life-on-life discipleship is not efficient, and it will bring all sorts of things to the surface as you begin to walk this out, yet this is the command of the Lord Jesus Himself.

> **Life-on-life discipleship is not efficient, and it will bring all sorts of things to the surface as you begin to walk this out, yet this is the command of the Lord Jesus Himself.**

Discipleship may be the most used and least agreed upon word in leadership circles, at least the ones I have been in for the past many years. Almost everyone believes that they are making disciples in ministry. However, for the purpose of this *recipe for reformation*, let me first start by simply looking at what Jesus Christ Himself gave us as His picture of discipleship. As I mentioned before, Jesus prayed all night to His Father when He began His ministry. Then He picked twelve disciples to lead and develop. Through discipleship, Jesus showed those twelve, and others who followed closely, what the Father was like. And He mentored them into their own identity as children of the Father.

Jesus did not do this from a stage or through a book. There was no printing press. Jesus wasn't handing out His books when He spoke. Many scholars believe that Jesus only did public ministry for eighteen months out of the three years, and I agree with them. Regardless of whether that opinion is shared, the question still stands, What did Jesus do with His disciples? I'm not asking what He taught or why He did the miracles that He did. I'm asking *how* Jesus lived His life with His disciples. What was His method of discipleship?

There are three things that stand out to me about Jesus' method of discipleship when I read the Scriptures. First, Jesus modeled a life of deep connection to His Father through prayer. Second, the Father led Jesus to shoulder-tap those He was assigned to disciple. And third, Jesus was not a peer of His disciples. He was their leader. Through humility, He led them in a life-on-life model by showing them how to love the Father and other people well.

I went to seminary to learn how to exegete the biblical texts, preach, and manage an organization. In contrast, Jesus made disciples, taught the kingdom, healed the sick, and delivered people of demons. I didn't learn any of that in seminary, and I don't know of a seminary in America that openly teaches a full context for what Jesus did. I'm sure there are some out there somewhere, but for the most part this is not the norm. Some of the greatest preachers and authors I have learned from over the years have loved God with all of their hearts and given away incredible intellectual capital, but they have not made disciples the way in which Jesus Christ did. I have been influenced by churches that love God tremendously, yet when you evaluate their model of discipleship, it's not what we find in the life of Jesus. Dallas Willard, one of the greatest thinkers and writers in the church in the last one hundred years, once said, "Every church has to ask two questions: 1) What is our plan for making disciples? and 2) Is that plan working?"

Cultivating Discipleship

If I wanted to, I could preach on Sundays and minister to some people throughout the week and call that ministry. However, with knowledge comes responsibility. When God opened my eyes to the non-biblical methodology of the church years ago, I started asking many questions and I am still asking questions. As I asked questions, I noticed certain trends in the church. For instance, I noticed that people prefer "connection groups" where everyone is received as a peer and where there is no clear leader modeling biblical discipleship. This is in stark contrast to a biblical *oikos* group with individuals who, because of righteousness in Jesus, are all equal in Christ, but who simultaneously honor the spiritual maturity evident in the person(s) leading the *oikos*. The disciple-maker is held accountable to Jesus to model Him, teach scriptural truth, and empower those being discipled, eventually releasing them to go do the same. I also noticed that people tend to reject any form or idea of spiritual authority, and that many define discipleship as someone teaching from a stage, classroom, or a book.

These may seem like overgeneralizations, but the trend of this reality has greatly increased in the past two decades, specifically with the church in the West. In fact, it has become an even greater trap thanks to the ease of digital communication that masks genuine connection. Jesus built a culture of discipleship in His ministry that was rightfully imitated in the early church. Take Paul for example—as he went on his three missionary journeys, we see him implement the same model that Jesus did. He traveled with an *oikos* (Greek word for the extended spiritual family) and raised others up. In my opinion, the most important thing that Paul ever did with his time was to disciple Timothy. Timothy would go on to become the leader of the church in Ephesus—the largest church in the world at that time. While Paul's letters and influence extend into the modern-day church, it's undeniable that he took the command of Matthew 28:19 seriously. This command hasn't changed. Those who consider themselves disciples of Jesus Christ are to go and make disciples.

It has been an uphill battle to establish a culture of discipleship over the past seven years at Bridgeway Church instead of an attractional model of ministry. Yet here we are seeing the fruit of what we have been contending for. The devil is not nearly as interested in the ministry of a powerful man or woman of God compared to a culture of discipleship. Discipleship makes the devil very nervous. Why? Because cultures of discipleship catch fire in a healthy way, making them more difficult to extinguish. When you study what's happening in Iran and China over the last two decades in the church, you see the underground church exploding because disciples are raising up other disciples. I see a day coming when the church in the West looks like what is already happening in these two regions.

> **This command hasn't changed. Those who consider themselves disciples of Jesus Christ are to go and make disciples.**

If cultures of discipleship were easy, most churches would be cultivating discipleship.

In today's church, most couples are searching out a community to connect with where they experience "belonging," instead of a married couple finding people of peace to disciple. A person of peace is someone willing to follow you and receive from you because you carry an undeniable spiritual maturity that they desire to grow into. They're not just interested in a lateral connection with you as a "brother or sister in Christ."

Is belonging bad? Nope. It's actually a core value we all have as humans. Is connection with like-minded people who are peers ungodly? Of course not. I'm just making the point that our personal priorities and perceived personal needs have kept us from engaging in a biblical mandate—and that's a problem.

Over the years, Wendy and I have learned that the only people we can truly disciple are those who are willing to receive from us. Although we all enjoy and long for community, it is undeniable that the strategy of finding people of peace is paramount when attempting to develop a culture of discipleship. Jesus Christ did not command us to go and find community. He commanded us to go and make disciples. This puts the attention on a person taking responsibility for what it actually means to disciple and be discipled. What if the only way that you knew you were a disciple of Jesus Christ was that you were actually making disciples? It's much easier to lean on the spiritual capital of someone on a stage, sow money from time to time into a church, listen to some podcasts or read some books on occasion, and count it all as a win than it is to disciple.

> Jesus Christ did not command us to go and find community. He commanded us to go and make disciples.

The more I read the Bible for myself, the more I realize that the model of the kingdom is intended to flow through the rhythm of a person making disciples through a life modeled in the home and not just in the "temple." I love Sunday gatherings, yet there is something supernatural when my wife and I have the people we are discipling in our home. It's much easier and safer to be a victim and blame a church, leader, boss, the past, or a plethora of other things for why we are not making disciples, than to actually jump into discipleship.

When you stand before the Lord Jesus one day, what excuse will you give Him for not taking the command of Matthew 28:19 seriously? I challenge you to ask yourself some serious questions right now. What steps can you take to make Jesus the Lord of your life today? What is it that you count as a success with what you are doing with your life? Do you value multiplication in the same way that the Father values it? Are you making disciples? If not, why is that? Is it possible that you are blaming another person or organization for why you are not multiplying through others? Is the neighborhood you live in actually an opportunity for you to pray about who it is that you should be discipling? Is your life worth imitating? What is God commanding you to do regarding biblical discipleship? These are hard questions, but I promise they are worth your time and attention.

Jesus Christ changed the world by discipling a few men. He picked the twelve men the Father led Him to disciple, and out of those twelve there were three Jesus focused on developing to a greater degree. I believe we will begin to see models of churches and marketplaces do the same.

I love seeing how God used Antioch as a base in Acts during the explosion of the early church, but I also notice something about Saul/Paul that helps us see the power of the *Home*. Before Saul's conversion, he was going into homes to persecute the church. Saul, also known as Paul, he continued to go into the homes, not to persecute the followers of Jesus but rather to spread the message of the Gospel.

Yes, Jesus also spoke in bigger gatherings around the temple and elsewhere, but discipleship was at the core of His ministry. I am not advocating that we stop gathering in large groups on Sunday or at other times. I believe that gathering in larger groups is a necessary and good expression for the church. However, we need to add the discipleship model to our expression of church in order to enter fully into God's recipe for reformation.

In this reformation of the church, we are not only going to see an increased priority on the *Tent*, we are also going to see a deliberate investment in equipping the everyday, non-vocational follower of Jesus into the *Home*. Homes will no longer be just the place where people sequester from the world. Homes will become houses of ministry in the everyday aspects of life. In our churches we need to hear and receive practical teaching on how to open up homes in the Name of Jesus for the purpose of making disciples.

> **Homes will become houses of ministry in the everyday aspects of life.**

Sunday school rooms and seminary classrooms have unapologetically used whiteboards to explain and teach in the name of equipping the believer. It is my hope and my belief that this reformation will include a value for learning the practical ways of discipleship and that this biblical value would be taught in the most academic of seminaries. I see the Father raising leaders who are willing to put the mission of His kingdom into the hands of ordinary people, to train them how to develop a system of multiplication in their everyday lives that will grow His church in a biblical way. Oh, that we would beware not to multiply pharisees in our churches and church leadership.

I believe that proof of this current reformation will be evident when we see the Bride of Christ collectively desire and value what the early church did by developing a true *oikos* out of the home, making disciples, and multiplying, thereby extending the reach of God's glory in the earth. I love having encounters with God. And I deeply value when God encounters are shared in large gatherings and undeniably experienced by many at one time. But what I have also come to value is training people to disciple. I love the biblical model of discipleship, and I believe it can transform the church and its impact in the world. God loves His church and won't leave us as we are now. He is transforming us to look like the early church that was composed of families with authority and structures that multiply. God is coming for His church.

Chapter 13

CITY: GOING INTO ALL THE WORLD

In 2016, while I was preaching at Bridgeway Church in Greenville, South Carolina, I stopped in the middle of what I was saying and yelled, "Bridgeway Church will not be a white church." I then prophesied strongly and passionately for a few minutes that God was coming to bring diversity to Bridgeway. Eleven o'clock on a Sunday morning in Greenville, South Carolina is the most segregated hour of the week in our city. You will have a hard time finding congregations that gather as faith families that don't look like each other. Greenville has come a long way since Dr. Martin Luther King, Jr. gave his life for equality and racial reconciliation, but if I'm being objective, the churches in this area don't reflect what that hero laid down his life for. We have white churches, black churches, Hispanic churches, and the list goes on. All of our children go to school together, but when it comes to faith communities, that is not the storyline for the most part. There is an exception to every rule, but for the most part this is the reality for the city in which I live.

When the death of George Floyd rocked America, I went into my basement and told the Father that I wanted to be a part of racial reconciliation in any way I could. As a result of that prayer, God first put a burden on me to pray, but it was months later that I realized that I was beginning to be a part of a much larger narrative that had been in the works for a very long time.

When I attended Beeson Divinity School, I developed a close relationship with a professor there named Dr. Robert Smith, Jr. Dr. Smith is not only the best African American preacher I've ever heard—he is simply the best preacher I've ever known. His book *Doctrine that Dances* won awards. When I was there, he became much more than a professor to me. For me and some of my classmates, he became a spiritual father. One semester we took a class from Dr. Smith called, "The History of African American Preaching." We studied the lives of so many great black preachers, and the only way I can describe what happened to me is that diversity exploded inside of me. I felt a literal call of God to be a part of a work for Him that would be very diverse.

God Builds the House

I met Wendy when I was twenty and in college. In my college apartment I had a large poster that said, "Give Racism the Boot." Wendy remembers in those early years of dating that even then I knew that God was calling me to steward something that would be different than white pastors going to a mostly white seminary. My relationship with Dr. Smith changed my life. It would be years before I realized just how prophetic that part of my journey was. As God would have it, I did not find that work of diversity—it found me.

One day as I was driving through Atlanta by myself, returning from preaching near Birmingham, I accidentally missed my exit. That's when I heard the Holy Spirit say, "Go to Dr. King's gravesite." I was only a few miles from where Dr. King is buried, so I drove over there. I sat down and looked at his grave, which is out in the middle of a pond. As soon as I sat down, a black man sat down beside me. There was no one else around, and if I am being honest, it scared me because he sat so close to me that I wondered if he were up to no good. He said to me, "Do you come here often?" I remember not even answering because I was trying to assess the situation. He then said to me, "Go read that plaque." As I walked over to read the plaque that described Dr. King's life, the man said to me, "You will lead them." After I read the plaque, I turned around and the man was not there. That was sixteen years ago.

Over the years since then I have often wondered what that encounter was all about. I have had some holy hunches along the way, but it has been in the past few years that it has all started to make more sense. In 2017, a visiting minister was on stage ministering at our yearly Table Conference and prophesied that God was bringing diversity to Bridgeway Church. When this minister gave that word, the Holy Spirit took me back to my time in college with Dr. Smith, who was the first spiritual father in my life. Then He reminded me of the encounter I had at Dr. King's grave. What began to happen shortly after is something that I did not see coming. I said yes to the call of diversity on Bridgeway Church.

Not too long ago, the Father began to press upon my heart that He was going to expand our vision to not only pay attention to but tend to more of the needs of the less fortunate in our area. God lead Bridgeway to start a food pantry ministry. We knew God's hand was all over it and it grew very fast. Most of the people we were reaching through the pantry were in the Hispanic community in the Greenville area. During this same time, I noticed that God was elevating the leadership of key leaders around us who were Hispanic. Over the last few years, God has brought some leaders to Bridgeway from all over who are Hispanic. The Holy Spirit kept saying to me, *"Unless the Lord builds the house, the builders labor in vain"* (Ps. 127:1). Mind you, I was not trying to do anything intentional toward diversity. God was building the house. It was happening so easily that it took zero effort on my part. I was building covenant community with people who loved the Lord as much as I do and they were not white, and praise God for that.

I slowly began to ponder what God was doing with what He has called me to lead, and that's when He told me to plant a garden.

Bridgeway Church sits on 35 acres on a beautiful piece of property. Over the last seven years, we have worked hard to maintain this property. Many people have told us how beautiful these grounds are. Before it was ours, the land belonged to Mt. Zion Fellowship. Forty years ago, God blessed them with this land and now He is blessing us with it. Many lives have been deeply impacted here on this property with the Gospel of Jesus Christ. I did not know until recently that the prophetic history of this land goes all the way back to the pre-civil rights days.

All of us, if we are faithful to the call of being a disciple of Jesus, stumble into our stories at some point or another. When I had the encounter at Dr. King's grave, I knew that there was something calling me to a life that would not look like the normal life for a white minister. God has slowly, and I mean slowly, unveiled His purpose for Bridgeway. For Heaven's sake, He named this church *Bridgeway* for a reason. He was and is making us a "bridge" between not only theologies, but races as well. The story I am about to tell shows that there is a narrative written over our lives before we are even born.

> **All of us, if we are faithful to the call of being a disciple of Jesus, stumble into our stories at some point or another.**

Cultivating Your Garden

After we started the food pantry, we noticed we had lots of food and supplies that blessed a lot of people, but we lacked fresh produce. Fruits and veggies can be quite expensive to buy and store, and so people tend not to donate them to food pantries. Instead of seeing this as a problem, we saw it as opportunity. We took a large chunk of land on our property and started a garden under the leadership of Bo Cable. Bo had experience in gardening because he led an award-winning garden in Greenville years before called Generous Garden. It is quite astonishing what God is doing through Bo's efforts as he grows produce for the poor in our Bridgeway garden.

The food pantry and garden fell into place here at Bridgeway because we had the vision, land, and the assignment to get this church out of the four walls of our building and go into our town. Years earlier I had cried out to God. "Father, I can't get us into the city. I don't know how. I want to serve the poor." God's response to my heartfelt cry was that He would help us, and He did. Here we are years later, and it's happening at a pace

I did not see coming. Another thing I did not see coming was the prophetic significance of the garden itself.

One day, I met a man in the garden named Fletcher and was instantly drawn to him. I had no idea how prophetic this meeting would be. Fletcher happens to be African American. He attends an all-black church right down the road from Bridgeway named Rock Hill Baptist Church. When Fletcher saw that we had started a garden, he walked down and began to help out from time to time. He was there when we dug an 800-foot well for water, planted beds, painted, tilled the soil, and all the other things that it takes to get a garden up and running.

Over time Fletcher and I got to know each other. Fletcher is retired and has lots of time to volunteer in our garden. In one of our many conversations, he said something that caught me way off-guard. Without knowing my passion for helping people walk in friendship with God, and without knowing that most of what I teach is about helping people walk back into what the Garden of Eden was supposed to be (which is deep connection with God), he looked at me and said, "You know this property was a garden before it ever became a church. Not only was it a garden, but it was shared between blacks and whites."

I got misty-eyed when Fletcher told me this because all along God has been leading Wendy and me to start a church called Bridgeway that has paradox at its core. God has burdened me with a driving passion to bridge gaps between theologies, races, methodologies, and ideologies to name a few. However, the burden in my soul is also matched with "God, I can't do this. I don't know what to do."

Fletcher then looked at me and said, "God is going to bring many different types of people to Bridgeway." As I sat there with him, I asked him to tell me the story of the land that the church is now on. He told me the names of the owners of the land and told me how his father was the one who worked in the garden for years. He said that not only was there racial peace between the families that owned the land but there was also so such an abundance of produce that they gave much of it away.

Here we are over fifty years later, and we decided to start a garden because we felt lead to do so. This garden has already created a culture where people of different races are not only working together, but we are getting to know each other. It's funny how produce can bring people together. This garden isn't just about fresh produce. This garden is playing a role in the healing of some of the people God has called here to Bridgeway. The garden is slowing us down to the rhythms of Heaven, connecting us to different people from different stages of life and different races, all while providing food to give away to the needy.

If we are honest, most people worship in cultures with very little real outreach. If you look at the life and model of the Lord's ministry in the Gospels, you see Him focused on the Father's presence (*Tent*), discipleship (*Home*), and outreach (*City*). At Bridgeway, we have seen the Father create a culture where whenever we have an opportunity to bless someone with a hug, a prophetic word of encouragement, or a prayer for healing—whatever the Lord leads us to do—we do it whether we are on Bridgeway property or out in the community. This recipe for reformation is about the church scattering outside the four walls. I think that is exciting!

God has burdened me with the desire to create a culture here at Bridgeway where reaching the needy outside of these walls is a driving passion. I was taking a walk with the Father one day when I saw in my spirit a T-shirt that said, "Gather, Scatter, Repeat." When you embrace God's recipe for reformation, He is faithful to bring leaders to you who have become people of peace who have a grace that extends into the *City*.

Here in the Greenville area God is using some key leaders in highly populated Hispanic areas from our church. People are literally being fed with food, born again, physically healed, and prophesied over. The plan is to continue to grow into the surrounding areas around Greenville. As I go forward, I am building relationships with non-white leaders and seeking to understand our differences and learning along the way that developing a culture of *City* in a church or organization takes a high level of humility and patience.

> God will not share His position in the hearts of His leaders with any other leader, especially a political leader.

Recently I preached at Bridgeway about the importance of humility as it relates to the ethnic diversity conversation. I gave Bridgeway an opportunity to repent of making any political figure their god in this past season. I began to prophesy that not only was Jesus Christ not a Southern white Republican, He is also not a liberal politician with any agenda that does not come from His Father. I believe it is so hard for people to relate to the Father on His terms because we tend to see God through a democratic lens when, in fact, He runs a theocracy.

Developing a City Focus

If your heart is open to allowing God to get you outside of the walls of your organization and truly serve the city you are in, you won't be able to do that if your political convictions outweigh your kingdom perceptions. God will not share His position in the hearts of His leaders with any other leader, especially a political leader. The Father is removing the idolatry of politics that has invaded His church. We will see leaders lend their sphere of influence into a higher Colossians 3 realm where they begin to set their hearts on things above more than on things below. Scripture tells us—no *commands* us—to first love God with all our heart, and then to love our neighbors as we do ourselves.

The point of going into the *City* has nothing to do with being project minded or even trying to meet some sort of Heavenly quota for service. It is a biblical model, a recipe for reformation. We are to take what is being imparted from the *Tent* and the *Home* into a place where hurting people need an embrace from the Father. It is about seeing our cities as mission fields. Any *Tent* or *Home* that does not have a *City* focus might appear holy, but it greatly lacks Jesus' biblical model of discipleship.

One of my favorite things that I do as a leader is listen to the stories of people who call Bridgeway home. Their stories tell me what God is doing in our city. I have noticed over the years that those who are overflowing with the heart of God are blessing others wherever they go. The church was never intended to be an organization that recruits people to join and stay inside the walls. In this reformation of the methodology of the church, not only are we going to see leaders lead their organizations toward the *Tent* and *Home* but also toward *Cities* as well. Although people tend to feel safer and more comfortable inside of a system that enables them to get connected, that is not the command of Jesus. We are all supposed to be making disciples and then scattering those disciples.

> God is extending you an invitation to be part of this. How will you RSVP?

Recruitment with no plan to multiply becomes like a pond that goes stagnant when there is no natural outflow. The inflow of God into our lives needs an outflow. Otherwise it will become stagnant. The church in the book of Acts was anything but stagnant. Relationship with the living God of all creation is anything but stagnant. Christianity is not a stagnant pastime. A life lived in the presence of almighty God, grounded in discipleship and rooted in outflow gives us a picture of the vibrancy of Heaven that God began in the Garden and intends to see implemented here on earth. God is extending you an invitation to be part of this. How will you RSVP?

Name Change

I have said many times over the past seven years at Bridge-way Church that my job is to look to what the Gardener is doing (see John 15:1-5). One of the truths which I also stand on is that unless God builds anything I have my hands on, it's all in vain anyway (see Ps. 127:1). Jesus Himself even said, "I only do what I see the Father doing" (see John 5:19). With that in mind, over the past year I have discerned that the Father is changing our name here in this community. This is not something uncommon in God's narrative. We see this in Scripture when He changes quite a few people's names. Abraham, Sarah, Jacob, Paul, and Peter are just a few who went through a transition in their destiny and name. I knew in my knower that God was changing our name here.

What sealed the deal for me was one day a prophet from New York City who was ministering at Bridgeway said to me, "The Father is changing the name of this church." I smiled and told him that I knew that, but I didn't know the name. That was until I asked the Father one day on the way home from a Sunday service what our name was and He said, "The Garden." Most of my encounters with God are not dramatic at all. This was one of them, and over the following months since God's confirmation of our new name, we began to see even the culture shift as the name became our identity. We simply want to help people walk in friendship with God, and in the garden that we are becoming we are seeing our new name define our new reality. In the midst of growing diversity, we are actually becoming simpler in our desire. We want to know Him, and He has made Romans 11:22 a plumb line for us. The Garden Greenville is a church that yearns to know Him both in His kindness and severity. The older I get, the more I realize that we are all on a journey. Bridgeway Church changed its name on the seven-year anniversary of its birth. There is so much drama and conflict from the promise God gives us into the reality of that manifestation. Great conflict typically precedes all of our destinies.

> **In the midst of growing diversity, we are actually becoming simpler in our desire.**

Perhaps that is where you find yourself in your current journey. Perhaps your theology is evolving, and the Father is taking you into a deeper perspective of who He is. I do sincerely pray that this book has helped you wrestle with some questions that need to be wrestled with. If Israel was birthed out of a wrestling match with God, then surely our stories will have times of great wrestling too. That is where the church currently finds itself. For such a time as this, may Paul's words guide you in your own journey with God: *"Therefore, my dear friends, as you have always obeyed—not only in my presence, but now much more in my absence—continue to work our your salvation with fear and trembling"* (Phil. 2:12).

Epilogue

RESTORING THE FEAR OF THE LORD IN THE CHURCH

W endy and I spent some time recently with Duncan and Kate Smith here at Bridgeway. Duncan and Kate are the leaders of Catch the Fire Network. They helped John and Carol Arnott steward what God did in Toronto for eleven memorable and life altering years beginning in 1994. Known to most as "The Father's Blessing," the move of God in Toronto saw and thousands upon thousands of people come from all over the world to be a part of how the Father was pouring Himself out on the church. I have so much honor for what Duncan and Kate mean to the Body of Christ.

As Duncan and Kate ministered to the staff at Bridgeway, I found myself weepy at God's goodness, full of gratitude as I watched two generals in the kingdom share a wealth of experience and impartation with the Bridgeway team. Throughout our few days together, the topic of humility kept coming up. The Holy Spirit manifested greatly, and as a teaching on the importance of humility flooded my soul, I shared the following with the staff in a time of prophetic swirl:

> The Father is the lowest of the low. Even though He is the Most High God, He is the lowest person to ever exist in His own heart. Humility is His middle name. In this coming move of God, the Father is going to raise unassuming leaders from unknown places who will be elevated in this season of the changing of the guard. I see a massive shift in the leadership of God's church globally. God made Adam from the dirt, and it's the dirty ones who will be elevated to lead this end-time move

of God. God is ripping the celebrity spirit from His church. He is placing the lowly ones at the helm to teach a generation how to raise disciples who raise disciples. He is creating models and cultures that see the habitation of Himself reside. The number one marker of this move of God will be humility. Those who see Him as the Most High God and fear Him above anyone or anything will be promoted in this season. *Humilitas* in Latin means "from the dirt." Those who stay in the dirt will find a high level of connection with God. The valley of Philippians 2 will mark this move of God. Get low and stay low. Stay low.

If you will be brave enough, you will see the fruit of the purpose of the journey of humiliation. From this pathway comes true humility. God is the only one who truly sees our hearts. May it be the cry of your heart to fear God above all else.

Recently I was reflecting on the story of Judas Iscariot and his betrayal of our Lord Jesus Christ. I lay in the bed and talked to the Lord about this. My mind raced to the Scriptures and Jesus began to show me things. One of the things He showed me is how often Judas called the Lord "Teacher." Yet the other disciples called Him "Master" a lot. The Lord began to show me how important it is to stay in a posture with Jesus as my master all the days of my life. While Judas was not incorrect in calling Jesus "Teacher," there was a lack of the fear of the Lord upon Judas that kept him from calling

Jesus "Master." All of the disciples were lacking in so many areas, yet it seems that those who kept Jesus Christ in His rightful position of master produced more fruit than those who did not.

None of us are self-made people. We all stand upon the shoulders of those leaders currently in our lives and those who have gone before us. Recently, Duncan and Kate Smith introduced Wendy and me to John and Carol Arnott. Years before, we had the privilege of hearing Carol, a giant in the faith, speak as we listened to her online. Her message on the fear of the Lord was a poignant insight into what the Father is currently doing in the church. Wendy and I gave John and Carol a big hug at the breakfast that was set up by the Smiths and thanked them for their contribution to the church, and specifically honored Carol for her courage to preach such a strong message on what is at hand for the church today. As we walk out our small part in this current reformation, Wendy and I are simply agreeing with what others have prophesied is coming, and in fact what is here now. I have done my best to share my thoughts and experiences on the current reformation in the pages of this book, and all I can say here at the end is, "So let it be, Lord Jesus."

> ## The fear of the Lord is returning center stage to the church.

The fear of the Lord is returning center stage to the church. A day is coming, and it is sooner than we think, when each of us will stand before Him and everything done while in the Body will be inspected by Him. Yes, for those of us who are in Christ, our sins are forgiven. Yet on that judgment day we will realize that our assignment was to be a reflection of our obedience to what He wanted for us here.

To fear the Lord means to obey the Lord. May you have a driving passion to fear the Lord to the last breath that you take on this earth. May you care about what He thinks more than anything else. And may you walk in an obedience that creates a draft for all those on your family tree, who are here now and who are not yet born, to come and catch.

In the Name of Jesus Christ our Lord, I pray that you play an active role in this reformation of His church with enough boldness to destroy any idols that are keeping you from a high level of connection with Him. May you live your life every day with the coming judgment seat of Christ in the forefront of your mind. And above all may your desire simply be to do the will of the One who is your Father.

Father, please take this book and use it to help a lot of people. We need You and we ask that You give us eyes to see what You see in this reformation. Come, Lord Jesus.

ABOUT CHAD NORRIS

Chad Norris is the senior pastor of The Garden in Greenville, South Carolina. He has a master of divinity from Beeson Divinity School and is currently working toward a doctorate at Regent University. Chad and his wife, Wendy, have three children and are passionate to create a culture of discipleship that begins in their own home and extends to everything they do.

To stay in touch with what Chad is leading:

www.thegardengreenville.com

www.jointheascent.com

www.coachandjoe.com

Coach and Joe Podcast

Do you want to discover more about who God is and who He is calling the Church to be? Visit us today at jointheascent.com and find resources, books, and coaching clinics that will help you walk in a deeper friendship with God.

We grow disciple makers who change the world.

LEARN MORE > WWW.JOINTHEASCENT.COM